Kerry V. Kern

Rottweilers

Everything About Purchase, Care,
Nutrition, Breeding, Behavior, and Training

With 21 Color Photographs
Illustrations by Michele Earle-Bridges

Consulting Editor: Matthew M. Vriends, PhD

BARRON'S

Photo Credits: Jane Donahue (Moments by Jane, Wellesly, MA): front cover; Gary W. Ellis: inside front cover, page 63; Dick Hamer: pages 27, 28, 46 top left; Rob Lauwers: page 46 top right; Wim van Vught: pages 9, 10, 45, 46 bottom, 64, inside back cover, back cover.

About the Author: Kerry Kern, formerly Managing Editor of the *Canine Graphic*, has written extensively on the subject of dogs. She is the author of *Labrador Retrievers, Siberian Huskies*, and *The New Terrier Handbook* (Barron's).

Advice and Warning: This book is concerned with buying, keeping, and raising rottweilers. The publisher and the author think it is important to point out that the advice and information for rottweiler maintenance applies to healthy, normally developed animals. Anyone who buys an adult rottweiler or one from an animal shelter must consider that the animal may have behavioral problems and may, for example, bite without any visible provocation. Such anxiety-biters are dangerous for the owner as well as for the general public.

Caution is further advised in the association of children with a rottweiler, in meetings with other dogs, and in exercising the dog without a leash.

All inquiries should be addressed to:
Barron's Educational Series, Inc.
250 Wireless Boulevard
Hauppauge, NY 11788

International Standard Book No. 0-8120-4483-5

Library of Congress Catalog No. 90-49829

Library of Congress Cataloging-in-Publication Data

Kern, Kerry V.
    Rottweilers : everything about purchase, care, nutrition, breeding, behavior, and training / Kerry V. Kern ; with illustration by Michele Earle-Bridges : consulting editor, Matthew M. Vriends.
        p.   cm.
    Includes index.
    ISBN 0-8120-4483-5
    1. Rottweiler dog. I. Title.
SF429.R7K47 1991
636.7'3 — dc20   90-49829
                                              CIP

Printed and Bound in China

4   4900   9

Contents

Preface 5

Before Buying a Rottweiler 6
Is the Rottweiler the Right Breed for You? 6
Purchasing Your Rottweiler 7
What to Look for in a Rottweiler Puppy 11
What Age Is Best? 12
The Purchase Agreement 12

Caring for Your Rottweiler 14
Helping Your Puppy Get Settled 14
    The First Day 15
    The First Night 16
Introducing the Puppy 16
Daytime Care 17
Puppy Socialization 18
Exercise and Housing Requirements 18
Traveling with Your Rottweiler 19
    Traveling by Car 19
    Traveling by Plane 20
Boarding Your Rottweiler 21
Protecting Your Rottweiler 22

Feeding Your Rottweiler 23
Types of Food 23
    Dry Food 23
    Canned Food 24
    Semimoist Food 24
    Home Cooking 24
Supplementation 24
The Feeding Process 25
Chewing 26

Grooming Your Rottweiler 29
Care of the Coat 29
Bathing 29
Care of the Nails 30

If Your Rottweiler Gets Sick 31
Evaluating Your Rottweiler's Health 31
    Eyes 31
    Ears 32
    Tooth Care 32
    Feet 33

Basic Medical Procedures 33
    Taking the Temperature 34
    Taking the Pulse 34
    Giving Medication 34
Vaccinations 35
Internal and External Parasites 35
    Worms 36
    Fleas 36
    Ticks 37
    Lice and Mites 37
Stinging Insects 38
Common Illnesses 39
    Vomiting 39
    Diarrhea 39
    Constipation 39
    Impacted Anal Glands 40
    Hip Dysplasia 40
Emergency Procedures 41
    Injuries 41
    Poisonings 42
Caring for Your Rottweiler as It Ages 42

Understanding the Rottweiler 44
History of the Rottweiler Breed 44
Behavior Patterns 47
Verbal and Nonverbal Communication 47
Communicating with Your Rottweiler 48
Living with a Rottweiler 49
The Working Rottweiler 49
The Quality Rottweiler 50
Rottweiler Standards 50
The AKC Rottweiler Standard 50

Training Your Rottweiler 54
Rules for the Trainer 54
Housebreaking 56
    Tips for Housebreaking Puppies 57
    Crating Your Puppy 57
    Paper Training 58
    Cleaning Up Waste 59
The Collar and Lead 59

Contents

The Basic Obedience Commands 60
   Sit 61
   Stay 62
   Heel 65
   Come 66
   Down 67
   Down-Stay 67
Training Problems 68

Breeding Quality Rottweilers 70
Selecting a Sire and Dam 70

Breeding Systems 71
   Linebreeding 71
   Inbreeding 72
   Outcrossing 72
Preparing for Breeding 72
Mating 72
Pregnancy 73
Delivery 73
Caring for Newborn Puppies 74

Useful Literature and Addresses 76

Index 78

Preface

At the end of every football season, popular sportscaster John Madden announces "The All-Madden Team" — those exemplary players that give the game their all and excel due to their perseverance and rugged determination to be the best. The 1989–90 team included its first mascot — "Cleat" Telchik — a rottweiler owned by a player on the Philadelphia Eagles. Madden singled him out as a "real manly dog . . . a dog you can be proud of." Rottweiler owners surely will agree with this summary.

It often is hard to separate fact from fiction when popular images of rottweilers are discussed. Rottweilers were cast as the ominous guardians of the devil in the movie *The Omen*, and they are often shown on television as snarling watchdogs lunging at fences in the hopes of catching some tasty intruder. Rottweilers commonly are portrayed as the brutes of the canine world — the champions of aggression. Such images make people unfamiliar with the breed cower at the sight of a rottweiler, and this notoriety does not do the breed justice. Unquestionably, the rottweiler deserves better.

As we begin the 1990s, the rottweiler ranks as one of the most popular breeds in the United States. According to American Kennel Club statistics, the rottweiler was the forty-fourth most popular breed in 1980, totaling 4,701 registrations. By 1989, the breed had skyrocketed to sixth place, with 51,291 registrations — an increase of 991 percent for the decade! Such sudden fame can be looked on both positively and negatively.

On the positive side, this growth attests to the wonderful, loving personality of the well-bred rottweiler. These dogs are devoted companions, and they excel in all aspects of the dog sport. Numerous rottweilers have won acclaim in conformation, obedience, tracking, and Schutzhund (guard dog work) competition, as well as in use as therapy dogs. They have proven themselves to be dependable, obedient workers and outstanding pets.

On the negative side, sudden popularity can create such an avid market for a "fad" dog that demand outpaces supply — and this can lead to unskilled breeders entering the scene in search of "easy money." Anyone who has ever raised and properly cared for a litter of puppies knows that this is not a get-rich-quick endeavor. Luckily, the rottweiler has thus far been protected from wide scale mass production due to the efforts of dedicated fanciers. For the sake of all involved, it cannot be stressed enough that anyone considering purchasing a rottweiler should investigate the puppy's background to be sure it stems from quality stock exhibiting the traits desired in this breed.

The material presented in this book provides a general overview of the breed. It is an introduction to many of the aspects of owning and caring for a rottweiler, and is not intended to delve into health topics that are best left to veterinarians or into behavioral problems that may require the expertise of a professional trainer. The book strives to portray the rottweiler, with both strengths and faults, as a wonderful breed, but not the breed for everyone.

I would like to acknowledge the assistance of my longtime friend, Matthew Vriends, PhD, consulting editor of the series, and Helgard Niewisch, DVM, who evaluated the manuscript.

K.V.K.

Before Buying a Rottweiler

Is the Rottweiler the Right Breed for You?

Purchasing a dog is a commitment that never should be taken lightly. Before you set out to select a new pet, evaluate your daily life-style in terms of how a dog will affect it. There are a few simple facts: a dog will need plenty of attention, exercise, and care over the next ten or more years. It must be well trained, well fed, and well loved if it is to thrive, and it must be welcomed by everyone in the home. Additionally, owning a dog is not cheap. Aside from the purchase price — which can be quite steep — there are basic expenses, such as food and licensing, as well as the necessary veterinary costs. In the case of a rottweiler, you can expect to spend as much as $100 per month on your dog. You may also want to consider purchasing liability insurance to protect against any possible damage done by the dog to others' property or person.

Clearly, dog ownership is a long-term commitment. Once you have given this some thought and are ready to proceed, there are specific aspects of your desired breed that must then be considered.

Reputable rottweiler breeders will be the first to tell you: *the rottweiler is not for everyone*. This is not to say that rottweilers make poor pets, are dangerous, or that this breed gets along poorly with people. That simply is not the case. However, this breed has special traits and requirements that must be considered carefully *before* the dog is brought into your home. Every prospective owner should understand the breed's typical characteristics, needs, and instincts and assess how they will mesh with those of the family.

The rottweiler has been assigned to the Working Group by the American Kennel Club. The breed traces its history back many centuries to progenitors that served as herding and hauling dogs in ancient Rome. The modern rottweiler is a rather large dog, standing from 22 to 27 inches (55.9–68.6 cm) at the shoulder and weighing from 80 to 135 pounds (36.3–61.2 kg). It is a very strong dog — even stronger than its rugged appearance suggests. From its days as a herder, the rottweiler inherits a protective nature and a tendency to "bump" its charges to get them back into line. Its compact musculature gives the full-grown adult enough power to easily knock a person over. This trait makes the breed a risky choice for families with small children or infirm or elderly adults. Although most typical rottweilers are gentle and tolerant enough to adapt to the antics of children, breeders suggest that children be *at least* school age before having a rottweiler as a pet.

Rottweilers possess great intelligence, unmatched loyalty, and a strong guarding instinct. They typically are devoted to their family, and often will bond very closely to one member. They thrive on companionship, so much so that they are prone to following wherever their master moves. Some owners cherish this devotion from their dog, others find it obtrusive at times.

If you are away from the home for long stretches of time and plan on leaving your dog unattended, this is not the breed for you. Similarly, the rottweiler does not thrive in a kennel situation and should be raised within the household, if at all possible.

A dog of this size and strength *must* be obedience trained. A rottweiler naturally is protective of its owner's property and if not tempered properly this territoriality can lead to an aggressive nature whenever outsiders are concerned. Although a rottweiler is not quick to bite, it may see fit to corner whomever it considers an intruder. Basic manner training should begin as soon as the dog is taken into the home, with formal obedience training beginning at approximately six months of age and continuing up until the point that the dog is able to reliably perform all the basic obedience commands (see Training Your Rottweiler, pages 54–69). The dog is considered reliably trained when it can be controlled by verbal command alone, no longer needing corrections with leash and collar. Many rottweilers exhibit a stubborn

Before Buying a Rottweiler

The well-trained rottweiler is a loving, trustworthy companion and protector.

streak, making obedience training all the more important and all the more protractive. If you are not willing to invest the amount of time needed to fully train your dog in proper behavior, the rottweiler is not the breed for you.

Although rottweilers have been raised successfully in apartment settings, they do require some vigorous daily exercise to remain in proper trim. Merely giving them access to a fenced yard is not enough. They need at least one lengthy walk daily, with a workout of some kind along the way. A rottweiler is not well suited to living with a sedentary owner.

Once you have thoughtfully considered these points, and decided that the rottweiler really is the breed for you, the hunt for your dog can begin.

Purchasing Your Rottweiler

At this stage, there are a few additional points to consider:

Do I want a puppy? Although a puppy certainly is adorable, a dog of this age requires an inten-

sive amount of attention and training. It must be housetrained, and will need almost constant supervision and guidance over the first six months or so. An older dog may be more suitable for some owners. However, older dogs will have had time to establish habits — ones you may not like and may find very difficult to correct!

Do I want a male or a female? A female rottweiler generally is smaller, calmer, and gentler than a male, and easier to train. All female dogs will come into season twice a year, which can cause some trouble if the dog is not spayed. Males, on the other hand, generally embody more breed instincts and traits: large size, great strength, more aggressiveness, and an overall robust nature.

Do I want a pet, a show dog, or an obedience competitor? How you intend to use your dog will affect where you go to find it. If you want a rottweiler destined for the show ring, you will first have to do some research into the breed standard to gain an understanding of how a show-quality rottweiler differs from the typical specimen of the breed. Only then will you be prepared to start evaluating potential dogs. If you are looking for an obedience competitor you will need to find a dog from a line that has shown good concentration powers and learning ability. If you are looking for a pet, your selection process will be somewhat less restricted, but will be just as important.

The American Kennel Club (AKC) and breed and show clubs are excellent sources for obtaining background information on the breed. The AKC publishes a monthly magazine, *Purebred Dogs: American Kennel Gazette,* which contains a bimonthly column on each breed as well as general information regarding dogs and their care. By writing to the AKC, 51 Madison Avenue, New York, New York 10010, you can obtain a list of the national rottweiler organizations and the name and address of the corresponding secretaries, as well as listings of kennels in your area. The AKC stresses, however, that this breeder information is supplied as a service to interested fanciers and

Before Buying a Rottweiler

does not imply an endorsement by the organization, which could not possibly evaluate every registered breeder.

When looking for a companion, or pet-quality, rottweiler, you have various options. The local kennels in your area that specialize in either show or obedience dogs also will have dogs for sale that do not meet the exacting requirements of competition. This does not mean that they are bad dogs; it just means that they are not expected to be champions because of some minor fault (a white spot on the chest, light eyes, a long coat, one or more missing teeth). Pet-quality dogs from kennels with good breeding practices are likely to be fine specimens of the breed, with sound temperaments and conformation. An experienced breeder will not randomly have paired any available male and female, but will have selected parents that were well suited for each other, and free from hip dysplasia and other inheritable disorders. You can expect to pay at least $600 for a pet-quality rottweiler.

At this time rottweilers are not bred on a large scale, so you may find it difficult to obtain one from a pet store. Should you be able to locate one, be sure to check into its beginnings. The main drawback from this type of arrangement is that you are unable to see or find out much about either of the parents. Some pet-store dogs are obtained from local breeders, but often they are purchased through brokers who contract with breeders elsewhere. Inquire into how the shop came to purchase the dog and what guarantees it will supply. A reputable shop will carry only healthy, happy puppies, and usually will decide not to carry a hard-to-stock breed rather than accept a poor specimen. You can expect to pay similar prices at a pet store as you would from a breeder in regard to pet-quality dogs.

You may have more luck purchasing a pet-quality rottweiler from a neighborhood owner who has decided to breed his or her pet. When considering a puppy from such a litter, be sure to check that both parents were registered purebreds

and that your puppy is eligible for registration with the AKC. If the owner cannot supply this documentation, then you must decide if this matters to you. The price for such a puppy should reflect the fact that you may not be purchasing a purebred animal.

Chances are slim that you would find a rottweiler in a humane society shelter, but should you locate one at such a facility be sure to do a thorough check into the reasons why the dog was placed there. There may be temperament problems that are not quickly visible with limited amounts of interaction with the dog.

If you are looking for a rottweiler destined for either show or obedience competition, you will do well to seek out a dog that has been bred specifically for this purpose. Many people involved in these sports spend years — often lifetimes — selectively breeding their dogs so that each new generation is as good as or better than the one that preceded.

Although a conformation show winner occasionally may stem from a neighborhood litter, most show dogs trace their roots to generations of carefully bred dogs. Selecting a puppy destined for the show ring is always a risky propostion. Rottweilers are slow to mature, with most coming into full bloom at around two years of age or later. Because most puppies are purchased at eight to ten weeks of age, selecting a show-quality rottweiler at this point is a best guess situation. It is quite common for show dogs to be purchased at a later age, such as six months, when they have matured a little and the breeder has been able to evaluate their potential more fully. You can expect to pay *at least* $900 for a show-quality rottweiler.

Top: A rottweiler dam needs a clean and spacious whelping area to safely accommodate her litter. Bottom: As these rottweiler puppies grow, their playful nature will lead them to explore beyond the confines of the whelping area.

Before Buying a Rottweiler

Finding a show contender is not easy. Show-oriented breeders often breed on a very limited scale, usually a few litters a year. You must understand thoroughly the requirements of the breed standard to be able to make any judgment about quality puppies. I would suggest that you attend several shows in your area, observe the puppies entered in the puppy classes, and ask as many exhibitors as possible for advice and if anyone has puppies available. An experienced, reputable breeder is generally the best judge of a puppy's potential, but there is no guarantee that a promising pup will grow into a show dog. I must also stress that dedicated breeders rarely will sell dogs they feel are top contenders to novices. They often will keep the best one or two for themselves or place them with experienced owner-handlers. There is a difference between show quality (a potential champion) and star quality (a potential best-in-show winner), however, and you should be able to purchase a ring contender if you put some time and effort into your search.

Although there are rottweiler kennels strictly devoted to obedience and Schutzhund (guard dog) work, fanciers interested in entering such competitions need not purchase dogs solely from such outlets. An obedience competitor needs a stable temperament, concentration, a sound physique, and the desire to work (but most importantly, a good teacher). These qualities should be found in any well-bred, well-socialized dog. One advantage of buying from a specialized kennel is that the puppy may have been highly socialized and indoctrinated since birth and encouraged to develop its instincts that would be useful in the sport.

◀ Given the proper balance of love and discipline, these rottweiler puppies will grow to be lifelong companions to their master.

What to Look for in a Rottweiler Puppy

When you have narrowed your search and are now considering specific litters of puppies, begin your evaluation by taking a hard look at the overall environment. The kennel or pet store itself should be a clean, warm place, free from parasites and odor.

Ideally, you should see the dam and perhaps even the sire of the litter. This will give you a fairly realistic image of how the puppy will mature in regards to size and coloring. The dam (mother) should never appear hostile or overly shy, as these are undersirable traits in the rottweiler. Acceptable behavior would be for the dam to act aloof, curious, or friendly toward you. Do not be put off if the dam appears slightly tired, thin, or out of shape. She has just been through a rough few months and her condition likely will reflect that. If you are concerned, you could ask the breeder for a prepregnancy picture of her. If the sire (father) is from the kennel and available for inspection, be sure to see how he interacts with the other animals. It is vital that both parents be stable emotionally and not prone to viciousness.

Inquire why these dogs were chosen for breeding, if they have been mated previously, and if they had been partnered before. If a previous litter has been produced by this pairing, ask to see any of the resulting puppies or, if they are no longer available, for the names and addresses of people who purchased dogs from the last litter. These puppies should be good indicators of how your puppy will mature.

The next step is to evaluate the litter as a whole. All the puppies should appear rugged and well nourished. Choosing the best puppy from a poor litter is always a gamble.

The rottweiler puppy should appear sturdy and big boned, with bright eyes, an alert expression, and a friendly, inquisitive nature. The coat should be glossy and pleasant smelling. A rottweiler pup should be fairly friendly and inquisitive and should not shy away from humans. Alternatively, it should not appear hyperactive. Watch how the puppy interacts with its littermates, and then remove it to a spot where it is with you alone. A well-socialized puppy will not be intimidated by this, although it may be a little reserved.

The rottweiler matures slowly and while young may appear out of balance at times. A veteran breeder will know best how his or her puppies may progress, based on experience with past litters. If conformation quality is important to you, it is vital that you select a breeder with proven credentials and a good reputation.

What Age Is Best?

Most dogs are purchased at approximately eight weeks of age. This is the optimal time for a puppy to be introduced to living solely with humans, as it is developmentally in what is known as the "human socialization period." From approximately eight to twelve weeks of age, the dog forms permanent bonds with those closest to it. If left confined with its dam and littermates at this age, a puppy will bond most closely with other dogs. If brought into a loving home, the dog will form a lasting human-dog bond.

It also is vital that a dog not be removed from its litter during the "canine socialization period" (birth through seven weeks). A puppy's dam plays an important part in the dog's life, as she establishes the first chain of command and teaches her young their first lessons in discipline. If removed too soon from its litter, a puppy will not have learned common behavior patterns and how to properly interact with others of its species. This could result in an adult dog that reacts in an overly aggressive or submissive manner when confronted with another animal. With a naturally powerful and aggressive dog such as the rottweiler, it is imperative that the dog be well socialized and able to interact with other animals in a controlled manner.

The greatest advantage of purchasing a puppy (besides being able to play with it during its most adorable stage) is that the owner is able to help shape the dog's character. The puppy learns a great deal during the first few months of life and an owner's influence is great at this point. However, a puppy needs an inordinate amount of attention and instruction during those first six months and an owner must be willing to make this commitment.

When purchasing an older dog, you will be faced with the fact that the dog has already formed its good and bad habits. Although this does not mean that they cannot be changed over time, it does usually mean that indoctrinating the dog to your way of doing things will not be as easy. However, acquiring a mature dog has some benefits, too. The dog should already be housebroken, will have had all its necessary shots, and should have gotten through the "wild" puppy days. When considering an older rottweiler, make sure the dog has been properly socialized to act agreeably around both humans and other animals, and that at least rudimentary obedience instruction has begun. As previously mentioned, rottweilers destined for show competition often are purchased well past eight weeks of age when their conformation can be more properly evaluated. Such dogs should not have been left to the confines of a kennel, however, but should have received ample human attention and socialization during those formative days.

The Purchase Agreement

Having selected the rottweiler that is best for you, you should finalize the transaction with a formal purchase agreement. This will list in writing all details of the transaction as well as the guarantee that the breeder will supply. The agreement must be signed by the seller and include the names and adresses of both purchaser and supplier, as well as all pertinent information concerning the dog: breed, sex, birth date, color, purchase price,

Before Buying a Rottweiler

and the names of the sire and dam (with AKC numbers, if available).

The types of guarantee will vary from breeder to breeder, but you should be allowed a specified number of days in which to return the dog should it fail a health inspection by your own veterinarian. Work out in advance how this type of situation will be handled: Is the money refunded, or is the dog replaced by another (at the breeder's or owner's discretion)?

The breeder should also supply the new owner with the AKC registration application, if you are purchasing a purebred. Most of the required information is to be supplied by the breeder, with the new owner listing the new address for the animal as well as two choices for the official name of the dog. It is the new owner's responsibility to complete the form, sign it, and return it with the proper fee to the AKC. If all is in order, the registration certificate should be mailed out in about one month.

You may find that the breeder will have further terms of sale. Many breeders will only sell pet-quality animals on the condition that the new own-

ers agree never to breed the dog. They often will withhold the dog's registration papers until they receive documentation that the dog has been neutered or spayed. Breeders do this as an attempt to improve the future generations by weeding out from the breeding stock all dogs with obvious physical or temperamental faults.

There often are terms involved when purchasing a show-quality dog. As previously mentioned, a dedicated breeder often will be unwilling to part with a quality dog unless given reassurances by the new owner that it will be used as intended. The breeder may choose not to totally relinquish control of the dog and may offer it to a purchaser only on a co-ownership basis. A breeder might stipulate that a dog *must* be shown in competition, or may require future rights to the breeding of the animal (having the right to use the dog in future breeding programs, having a say in future breedings, or requiring a pick from a future litter). By signing such a written agreement, a new owner is bound to follow these terms, so be sure of all the implications of this procedure before agreeing to them.

Caring for Your Rottweiler

Proper care for a rottweiler involves more than feeding, grooming, and housing the dog. Albeit these basic requirements certainly must be met— now and for the next nine to eleven years—owning a rottweiler brings with it a greater than average amount of responsibility. An owner must be aware of the breed's special qualities and must work actively to shape and enhance the dog's natural abilities. This means providing an abundance of affection, exercise, and obedience instruction from the dog's first days in the home. A puppy will then get a good start in life, which is the key to having it grow to its fullest potential as a trusted companion in the home.

Helping Your Puppy Get Settled

When you welcome a rottweiler puppy into your home, you are asking it to adapt to living in your "human pack," which comes complete with a new set of rules and experiences. With plenty of love and attention, your rottweiler should make the transition from its litter to its new home with ease and emerge in later years as a calm, loving companion. The owner must control the situation from the start and provide the necessary guidance that will produce a loyal, obedient, and properly socialized dog.

Prepare for your new puppy's arrival by stocking up on the essentials *before* bringing it home. You will need:
• food and water bowls (select ones that are heavy enough not to slide while the dog is eating or drinking);
• a high-quality puppy food (preferably the brand it has already been eating);
• a crate or some appropriate bedding;
• a well-fitting collar;
• a training lead;
• a bristle brush and hound glove; and
• a few sturdy chew toys.

Your rottweiler puppy has a curious nature, and it can get itself into plenty of trouble if the house is not "puppy proofed." All items that can be chewed or swallowed should be removed, and you should check for any heavy items that are stored low enough to fall on the puppy. Be sure all electric cords are secured, as a teething dog may try to chew on them. Close off all open staircases to insure that the puppy will not fall down the stairs and injure itself. It may sound foolish, but the best way to spot potential dangers is to get down on your hands and knees and inspect each room from the puppy's perspective.

During the first few days in a new home, the puppy gets its first lessons on life with the new owner in the new territory. These first impressions can be lasting ones, so make sure these early days are enjoyable and informative for the puppy.

Monitor the puppy's actions and movements at all times. This will keep the dog from getting overly excited or nervous, and will protect it from becoming exhausted or being injured. One of the most common injuries to a puppy occurs when it is allowed to roam and is later stepped on while under foot. An overly exhuberant puppy can jump recklessly from too great a height and the end result can be a broken leg, hip, or shoulder. Constant supervision helps the puppy control itself and helps the owner indoctrinate the new houseguest to the rules of the home.

Discipline must begin as soon as the rottweiler puppy reaches its new home. The puppy probably has never lived strictly with humans before, so it will have to learn that life in this new pack involves corrections and discipline, as well as lots of love and fun.

Many new owners believe that a puppy cannot learn while young or that trying to get a puppy to obey at an early age will ruin its spirit. Both of these notions are inaccurate. The puppy's dam already has made it perfectly clear to her pups that there are limits to acceptable behavior and when rules are broken there is a correction. The owner must step into this leadership position.

The puppy will learn a lot about basic manners during the first days and weeks in its new home. A puppy is a keen observer of body language and it

Caring For Your Rottweiler

If your grown rottweiler is not to be allowed on the furniture, you must begin teaching that this is not acceptable from the time the puppy enters the household. Issue a firm ''No!'' as you point to the floor. Assist the dog to the floor if necessary.

will know when its owner is displeased. The trick is to get the puppy to understand what it has done wrong, and then show it the proper action. Corrections at this age should be gentle but firm and almost always can be handled by a quick, verbal scolding. When the puppy corrects its misdeed, shower it with praise. Your rottweiler soon will be striving instinctively to receive more praise, and this desire will form the basis for all future learning experiences.

The First Day

The first day in a new home needs not be overly traumatic if handled properly. It is vital that you supply the puppy with plenty of love and attention during the first few days. Arrange to pick up the puppy when you have several days free to devote to welcoming the puppy to its new home. If you bring a puppy home one day and then leave it

alone the next while you go to work or school, the puppy may feel abandoned and subsequently may have a difficult time adjusting. Try to pick the puppy up in the morning, as this will leave you the entire day to make it feel welcome before it must face its first night away from its dam and littermates.

A rottweiler puppy is an adorable clown, so it is only natural for you to shower it with love and affection. The more affection and praise you give, the more reassured and comforted the puppy will feel. Speak to the puppy in soft, low tones and treat it gently. You will be a less frightening and more lovable figure if you get down on the floor and play with the puppy on its level. Though hard to resist, rough play is not recommended during the first few days when you are trying to establish a leadership position and the puppy is trying to figure out where it ranks in its new pack.

Show the puppy where its food and water bowls are located as soon as you get home, and

When lifting a rottweiler puppy, be sure to support it properly. Place one hand under the puppy's rear end and the other around its rib cage.

then take it to the elimination area. It's never too early to start housebreaking! Finish the tour by showing the dog its sleeping quarters. You can then let it roam about and explore on its own — with you monitoring from close by, of course.

The puppy will soon need food. To help avoid a possible case of upset stomach in the already excited dog, cut the normal ration by about one-third. You can resume full rations once the dog appears to have settled in a bit. Afterward, the puppy may want to explore some more, or it may settle down for a nap.

Until approximately 20 weeks of age a rottweiler puppy will need frequent rest periods. It will exhibit great swings in energy levels. Periods of great activity will be followed closely by periods of sound sleep. The puppy will need its own sleeping area as well as a small bed, sleeping box, or crate (see more on crates in Crating Your Puppy, page 57). This will form the pup's new "den." Bring the puppy to this area whenever it seems to be tiring.

The First Night

The first few nights away from dam and litter-mates most likely will be frightening for your puppy. It may whimper or cry and will need some comforting, but do not overdo it. If you bemoan the fate of the "poor little puppy" it may decide from hearing you that there *really is* something to be afraid of. At bedtime you should exercise the puppy, bring it to its sleeping area, pet it and talk soothingly to it for a few minutes, and then go.

Although that routine may sound a bit hard-hearted, it is important to establish a routine right from the start and stick to it. This will set the pattern for the nights to come. If you don't want your dog sleeping on your bed or in your room in the future, don't begin that pattern the first few nights. Consistency is vital and it helps the dog learn to trust and understand you. Because of this, you cannot allow the puppy to do something one week that is forbidden the next.

Making the nighttime routine seem matter-of-fact will be more helpful for the puppy than if you draw it out. If the puppy raises a fuss, return after a few minutes and reassure it once more, but *do not linger there or remove the puppy from the sleeping area*. Picking up the puppy will encourage it to continue this behavior, as it will learn that if it howls long enough you will come and get it.

A puppy usually will settle down quickly if you place a hot water bottle under its blanket to imitate the mother's warmth and play some soft, soothing background music. This may relieve the puppy's tension enough to have it fall asleep.

Remember to praise the puppy and lavish lots of attention on it first thing each morning to reward its good behavior during the night. Although the first night or two may seem excruciating for all involved, things quickly will settle into a pattern and everyone soon should be sleeping soundly through the night.

Introducing the Puppy

It is easy for everyone to get caught up in the excitement of having a new puppy in the home, but try not to allow the puppy to get overstimulated. The first few days should be fun, but not exhausting. Even your rough and tumble rottweiler will need to take things slowly. Learning the voice and appearance of the members of the immediate family is the puppy's first chore. Make things easy during the first days by not exposing your rottweiler to a continuous stream of new faces anxious to meet the new puppy.

Each rottweiler is an individual whose responses will vary from dog to dog. As a rule, it is easier to integrate a puppy into a household, whereas an adult is slightly less adaptable. Adult rottweilers usually are least tolerant of other adult dogs of the same sex. Introducing a rottweiler into a household already containing an adult of the same breed often can be difficult, but can be controlled with obedience training and praise. If your dog lives in a one-dog home, it is vital that it be exposed to as many other dogs as possible on a routine basis so that it grows up well socialized.

Most rottweilers are very tolerant and loving toward children, but some do not adapt well to the rough treatment children can inflict. When there are young children in a household, all meetings with the puppy must be monitored closely. The children must be taught how to gently pet, lift, and handle the puppy. Should the puppy get excited by the children's high-pitched squeals, it may try to nip at them (as it would a littermate), so be sure to correct it with a sharp "No!" Adult rottweilers will sometimes bump into children, usually in an effort to move or "herd" them. An adult rottweiler easily can knock a young child over, so it is best for an adult person to be present at such meetings. Because of this, some breeders recommend that rottweilers not be placed in homes with young children.

Before you introduce any other pets in the home, try to give the puppy a little time to get its bearings. The other pets surely will sense the new presence, however, so the delay should not be for long. All the pets must strictly be supervised and restrained. Well-trained adult rottweilers should be expected to react peaceably toward a puppy, but you must be prepared for an unfavorable response by having them on lead. Praise all the dogs throughout the meeting, giving the adult lavish amounts of affection and attention. If any of the animals growl menacingly or lunge at the other, immediately correct with a stern warning, a shake of the neck, and remove the offender from the room. A new puppy is sometimes thought to be a threat to the household order, and the animals will need to work out a new pecking order, but this competitiveness should ease over time if handled properly. Be sure to give equal amounts of affection to all pets in the home to avoid unnecessary competition. Do not try to always keep the animals apart, as this will enhance any existing tensions between them.

A rottweiler may exhibit some aggressive behavior toward cats. Because dogs and cats do not understand each other's body language, their reaction when they meet can be unpredictable. A rottweiler that has been raised with cats generally will be tolerant toward them throughout its life.

Daytime Care

A rottweiler puppy will need a lot of attention from day one. The impish puppy grows into the powerful adult, and it needs strong guidance and companionship throughout that growing period. A rottweiler should not be left alone for great lengths of time, as it undoubtedly will feel abandoned (and most likely it will take this frustration out on your furniture, trees, or personal property).

Most maladjusted adult dogs began as lonely or poorly treated puppies, and the effects of a poor beginning can be devastating. With a breed such as the rottweiler, the puppy must be closely monitored and encouraged so that the positive breed traits—loyalty, affection, obedience—become pronounced and the potential negative traits never develop. A well-bred puppy exposed to periods of loneliness and abuse can develop into the high-strung, aggressive rottweiler characterized in television shows or popular movies as the monster behind the chain fence that lunges at all who pass by. Those poor creatures are created by poor owners, and dedicated rottweiler breeders and owners can wipe out that image by making sure their dogs get a good start.

If you must leave the home for an extended length of time, try to take the puppy with you. If this is not possible, arrange to leave the dog with someone it is acquainted with.

There are some facts of life that all dog owners must face: a puppy has exercise, elimination, and socialization needs that must be attended to during the day. In today's society, most families now have two wage earners. Does this mean that no one who works should own a rottweiler, or that we are doomed to a generation of neurotic dogs because no one is home during the day to teach them? No, it means that such owners will have to make arrangements for their puppy during the time they will be absent.

As the dog matures, it will be able to be alone for longer periods, but while it is young you may need to hire someone to care for your puppy. In many cities there are professional "dog walkers" or "sitters," and retirees or homemakers often are willing to come to your home and care for your pet. Alternatively, you may be able to find someone who will watch the puppy in their home during the day to avoid any extended separations. If you cannot attend to this particular need, do not consider owning a rottweiler.

Puppy Socialization

Socialization for your rottweiler should begin while the dog is quite young. It should be exposed to as many situations as possible, and regularly should meet and interact with other animals and unfamiliar people.

Puppy socialization classes, often called Kindergarten Puppy Training (KPT), are informative sessions held by local dog clubs to help introduce both owner and puppy to some basic training and discipline techniques. These classes do not include formal obedience training, but instead focus on showing owners some basic handling skills and housetraining methods. The instructors discuss canine nutrition and health care and provide background information on how a puppy learns and understands.

KPT classes also are valuable for new owners of rottweilers. The sessions attempt to teach various techniques for establishing leadership and gaining control over the puppy right from the start. The emphasis is on effective communication, and the trainers show owners how to behave in a manner their puppy will understand. When a dog does not receive the cues it expects from a leader, it does not feel compelled to obey. Puppy socialization classes help produce more effective owners, as well as well-mannered puppies.

KPT classes also are valuable because they expose the puppy to new people, dogs, and surroundings. They give owners experience at having their dog encounter unfamiliar dogs. In this way owners learn how their dog instinctively reacts in these situations, and they can then know how to control or enhance this type of reaction. Such a lesson can shape the course of how the dog will interact with strange animals when it is an adult.

Puppy socialization classes help the dog learn self-control and how to handle new situations. This is confidence building. Such classes can instill a sense of accomplishment in the dog, and this paves the way for the dog to have a lifelong positive attitude toward the training process.

Exercise and Housing Requirements

The rottweiler was developed as a working breed, and it therefore requires some regular vigorous exercise to keep in trim and proper spirit. It

Your rottweiler should be allowed plenty of time outdoors, but these exercise periods must *always* be in a fenced-in area or with the dog on leash.

seems to bloom when given a chance to participate in some activity with its master.

Although rottweilers have been kept successfully in large apartments, they do best in homes with access to a large yard. The yard should be fully fenced to a height of 6 feet (1.8 m). Puppies in particular need to get out in the yard each day and work off some of the abundant energy they pack in their powerful frame. A well-exercised puppy is much less likely to involve itself in destructive chewing or digging.

Rottweilers usually are content to spend a considerable amount of time outdoors, but they must always be provided with protection from the elements. The breed does better in a cool or temperate zone, rather than in an excessively hot area. Because of their black coat color, rottweilers are prone to heat stroke if left outside in the direct sun during hot weather.

The rottweiler should be provided with a doghouse to supply adequate shelter against heat,

A well-constructed doghouse provides ample protection from both heat and cold. A hinged top such as this allows the house to be easily cleaned.

cold, and dampness. It should be large enough to allow the dog to fully stretch out, but not so large that it will not retain heat during cold weather. The entrance should be just large enough to allow the dog to enter easily. A doghouse with a hinged top is easiest to clean.

Place the house in a shaded area during the hot months and in a sunny spot during cold periods. The house should be mounted on platform risers or placed on blocks to stand several inches off the ground, thereby avoiding direct contact with the soil. Do not position the house directly against a fence. Although rottweilers are not noted climbers, placing a doghouse against a fence gives an excited dog the opportunity to climb upon it and jump the fence.

Traveling with Your Rottweiler

Most rottweilers enjoy traveling with their master, especially if the other choice is staying home alone. In fact, it is terrific socialization for the dog to experience as many new situations, sights, and sounds as possible.

Traveling by Car

Begin familiarizing the dog with riding in the car from the time it is a puppy. The dog should always be placed in the back seat. When the car is in motion, it would be safest for the dog to ride in its crate. Many people find this too cumbersome, however, and instead teach their dog to lie down during the ride. If your car or van is large enough to have open space at the back, you can purchase a dog grill to partition off an area for the dog.

To improve air circulation during warm weather, keep the car windows open approximately 2 inches (5.1 cm). Specially designed window screens that allow the window to be opened more widely can be purchased if you travel frequently without air-conditioning during hot weather.

Rottweilers can be overcome by the heat, so during hot periods provide the dog with a small amount of water at regular intervals when traveling. Never leave a rottweiler unattended in a parked car during the heat of the day. The temperature inside a parked car can soar in just minutes and prove fatal to the dog. Puppies especially are susceptible.

Never allow the dog to hang its head out the window while the car is in motion. This can result in eye, ear, and throat injuries. Also, the dog may lunge against the window in reaction to something it sees, possibly escaping or being injured in the process.

Do not feed the dog for approximately four to six hours before leaving on a long trip in the car, as a full stomach can often lead to motion sickness. A small amount of water is permissible before the trip.

If your rottweiler is prone to vomiting in the car and you are planning an extended ride, consult with your veterinarian regarding medications, but use them with caution. Most dogs will outgrow a tendency toward motion sickness as they get more accustomed to trips in the car, so medicating the dog should be unnecessary. The primary effect of tranquilizers is to make the dog drowsy; they don't minimize the dog's physical discomfort. In fact, tranquilizers inhibit the dog's ability to regulate body temperature, and this could pose problems for rottweilers that are already heat sensitive.

Plan on stopping every two hours on long trips to allow the dog to relieve itself, have a drink, and get some exercise. Always keep your rottweiler on a leash during such stops, as it may become spooked by the unfamiliar terrain and bolt away or toward something it sees in the distance.

On long trips requiring overnight accommodations, be sure to make arrangements *in advance*. Most hotels and motels will not allow dogs. Travel guides or your local automobile club may be able to supply you with a list of places along your route that will allow animals.

To help reduce the chance of digestive problems during your trip, be sure to bring along an adequate supply of the dog's normal food. The dog already is faced with many new and unusual conditions during a trip by car, so a constant diet becomes an important stabilizing factor.

Traveling by Plane

Over the last decade travel by air has become much safer for animals, but it still can be a harrowing experience for your dog. Although government regulations have forced the major airlines to better protect the animals in their charge from extremes of temperature and mishandling, the owner should take precautions as well. The first step is to have the dog checked by a veterinarian to verify that it is in good health. A health certificate issued within 30 days will be required by most commercial airlines.

Book your dog's flight with its convenience — not yours — in mind. Late night or early morning flights will ensure that the dog is not waiting as cargo on the runway and baking in the midafternoon sun. There are various types of passage that you can book for the dog (checked baggage, cargo, or priority cargo), and the prices vary consid-

When preparing for air travel, the crated dog may be loaded on a dolly for easy transportation.

erably. Do your best to get the dog on a nonstop or at least direct flight. There is an added risk of the dog being misplaced or injured if it must be moved around to make connecting flights. If your dog must travel on connecting flights, arrange to break up a long trip with a rest stop. Many airports have arrangements with kennels and transport organizations for this purpose. Your dog will benefit greatly from such an arrangement.

Place the dog in an airline-approved crate for shipping. It only should be large enough for your rottweiler to stand in and turn around. Most airlines will furnish owners with suitable crates for shipping their dogs, for an additional charge and if contacted in advance. Crates also can be purchased from pet supply shops. Dogs that already are accustomed to a crate will be less stressed than first timers. If possible, allow a newcomer to spend some time in the crate before taking the actual trip.

Clearly mark the outside of the crate with "Live Animal," the dog's name, and the name, address, and phone number of both the sender and recipient. Tape another copy of this information on the inside of the crate with the dog. If the dog is taking any medication, be sure that it is marked clearly as well.

Place some soft, absorbent bedding or a blanket at the bottom of the crate for the dog's added comfort. Enclose a nylon bone to help alleviate tension and boredom during the trip. Be sure the plastic water dishes are in place near the bars of the windows when the dog enters the crate. However, do not fill them with food or water before departure, as this invariably will spill and make the trip uncomfortable for the dog. An attendant will be able to pour water for the dog without having to open the crate, should the need arise. A supply of the dog's normal food also should be sent along to help avoid digestive upsets when the dog arrives at its destination.

Many novice shippers make the mistake of sedating their dogs before an air flight. Although it is true that a nervous dog can panic and injure itself during flight, it is better to teach the dog to relax in the crate rather than sedate it. Tranquilizers can depress respiration, and this factor — when combined with excessive heat and oxygen reduction, which are common conditions during air flight — can sometimes lead to heat stroke and death.

Withhold food for eight to ten hours before the flight, and be sure that the dog is exercised just prior to entering the crate. A soiled crate will make the dog very uncomfortable during the flight.

Be sure to check with the airline prior to departure for instructions on how to board the dog. Stay with the crate for as long as possible and ask to see the holding area. Speak with every airline official connected with the flight you can find, telling them what is in the crate and where it is going. You often can find the person who is in charge of loading the crate and express your concern about the dog's care. Be sure you have all information on the dog written down for the person who will be receiving the dog, including a tracking number.

Verify with officials in charge of the loading process that the dog has, indeed, been loaded on the plane and confirm that the flight has left before you leave the airport. Should there be an extended delay after the dog has been loaded on the plane, ask that the cargo door be opened. Should the flight be cancelled, you will need to be there to make new arrangements for the dog.

Boarding Your Rottweiler

When you must travel and cannot bring the dog along, you will need to find good accommodations for it. The best solution is, of course, to have someone the dog already knows take care of it. If this is not possible, make an effort to find a caregiver who is familiar with rottweilers. A logical place to start is with the dog's breeder, if in your area. Many breeders will temporarily board animals. Not only are they familiar with your dog, but who better to trust than someone versed in the particular requirements and traits of rottweilers?

Some veterinarians have boarding services, as do commercial kennels. Most of these establishments are well run, clean, and attentive to the dog's basic needs. You can expect to pay from $14 to $20 per day. Be sure to visit and inspect the kennel beforehand. Ask about the daily exercise routines and feeding procedures and check that the boarding kennel is accredited by the American Boarding Kennel Association (ABKA). A list of approved kennels in your area can be obtained by writing the ABKA at 4575 Galley Road, Suite 400A, Colorado Springs, Colorado 80915.

Whatever method you use, always leave enough of the dog's normal food to last until you return.

Protecting Your Rottweiler

A sad side effect of popularity has been the number of thefts of rottweilers in recent years. A number of animal protection agencies have issued a warning that dognapping is on the increase. It may seem hard to imagine that a stranger would attempt to steal a rottweiler from its home or yard, as a rottweiler's natural protective instincts and loyalty to its home usually are so well developed that it usually would try to corner any stranger who would enter its domain, but it does happen.

Some rottweilers are more affable than others, and professional thieves often employ elaborate methods to restrain or entice a dog (such as parading a bitch in heat near an eager male). You can help protect your dog by never leaving it unattended outside the home.

It is a good idea to have your rottweiler tattooed. This is a relatively painless procedure that can be performed by most veterinarians for a nominal fee. Many dog clubs also hold annual clinics to perform this service for dog owners. The use of tattoos is endorsed by dog organizations, and show competitors are not penalized for having a tattoo.

The tattoo will be a permanent aid for identifying the dog should it become lost. It also will prevent the dog from being sold to research laboratories that sometimes purchase "strays."

In most cases, the dog's AKC registration number or the owner's social security number is tattooed onto the dog's inner thigh. The inside of the ear also can be used, but there have been cases where a dog's ear has been cut off to remove the tattoo. The registration number is preferred over an owner's social security number, as the dog may have more than one owner during its lifetime. The tattoo number should then be listed with one of the national registries, which will record for an annual fee all pertinent information on the dog and owners.

Feeding Your Rottweiler

Rottweilers are large, active dogs with high energy needs. Most have great appetites and will eat whatever they are given. Feeding such dogs sounds like a simple — although potentially expensive — process, but because feeding does have a direct effect on a dog's health and longevity, it should not be taken lightly.

The following are a few basic rules that help protect your dog from problems related to feeding:

• Wash all food and water bowls daily in hot, soapy water to prevent the growth of bacteria.

• Have ample amounts of clean, fresh water available at all times, especially during periods of hot weather.

• Remove the water bowl at night if the dog is having housebreaking problems.

• Vary the diet only when absolutely necessary.

• Introduce a new food slowly, mixing it with the old, to avoid digestive upset.

• Bring along a supply of the dog's usual food when traveling or whenever the dog must be kenneled so that it does not have to suddenly adjust to a new food.

Types of Food

There are various types of food you can feed your rottweiler. Some dog owners select one type; others use a combination. The task is to present a daily ration that nutritionally is complete and balanced and suited to your dog's particular lifestyle. Which type of food is best? Which brand is best? The owner must take many factors into consideration, and then do some comparative shopping, when making this decision.

Dry Food

On an ounce for ounce basis, dry food (commonly referred to as kibble) is the least expensive and most popular type of prepared dog food. On average, a rottweiler will eat between 15 and 25 pounds (6.8–11.3 kg) of kibble each week. Given

that in 1990 a 20-pound (9.1 kg) bag of high-quality dry food costs approximately $17, the expense can be considerable over a lifetime!

There are many brands and formulas of dry food on the market. Most are composed of a type of cereal, soy, water, meat by-products, and a small amount of fats, vitamins, and minerals. Select only those products labeled "nutritionally complete," but bear in mind that this label should not be the only determining factor.

The exact formulation of the product determines how much of the food the dog must eat in order to fulfill its dietary needs. Read the suggested feeding amounts per weight of dog as listed on the package. The least expensive brand of kibble may, in the long run, not be the best buy as the dog may have to eat more of it than it would a premium dry food in order to fulfill its dietary requirements.

Ingredients in the less expensive dry food brands can vary from batch to batch, as fluctuations in the availability of the base crop (soy, corn, barley) cause the manufacturer to vary its blending at various times during the year. The premium meat-meal based kibbles sold in pet shops are designed to offer a stable mixture from batch to batch that nutritionally is complete, easily digested, and formulated to help produce a firm stool. Although these premium dry foods may cost a little more on a per pound basis, the superior quality guarantees that the dog will fulfill all its nutritional requirements without having to eat massive amounts of the food or receive supplementation.

Active dogs such as rottweilers need a diet that can fulfill their energy demands. Because dry food products can be low on fat content, owners can boost the fat by adding approximately one-half can of canned food or several tablespoons of oil to the kibble.

To make the kibble more palatable for the dog, and possibly avoid a digestive condition called bloat, saturate the food with warm water until it is soupy and let it stand for approximately 30 minutes (refrigerate the food while soaking during hot weather). Stir the remaining "gravy" around the kibble before serving. By preparing the food in this manner, it will absorb most of the moisture and expand before the dog eats it. It is also wise to feed the dog only after it has been inactive for 30 minutes, and to keep the dog's activities limited for one hour after eating.

Canned Food

Many owners mistakenly believe that because canned food is more expensive than dry food, it must be better. Although canned food is the food highest in protein, too much protein in a diet is not better than just enough protein. Most canned dog foods contain more than 75 percent water. The remaining components are meat by-products, soy fillers, vitamins, minerals, and, frequently, artificial coloring and preservatives.

When reading the label of a canned dog food, bear in mind that the first four ingredients are the primary components. Avoid products that contain high levels of red dye, salt, corn syrup or sugar, and preservatives. The high water level and additives in canned food can have a diuretic effect on many dogs.

Canned food should comprise no more than one quarter of a rottweiler's daily intake, and it should be mixed with a high-quality dry food for best results. The canned food products formulated for the various stages of life are most recommended. Because canned food is highly palatable, dogs needing to gain or maintain weight can be fed higher levels of this food. Conversely, overweight dogs should be given very limited amounts of canned food.

Semimoist Food

The pouches or "hamburgers" touted for their convenience are the most expensive type of dog food. These semimoist foods contain approximately 25 percent water and are composed primarily of soy meal, meat by-products, and cereal.

They also contain additives and preservatives, although the concentration of sugar and salt has been decreased in recent years. Semimoist products are highly processsed and high in calories, and some dogs have experienced various types of allergic reactions — from skin biting and scratching to hyperactivity — in response to the preservatives.

Semimoist foods should comprise no more than 25 percent of the diet and should be used in combination with a high-quality dry food. Semimoist products are very popular with most dogs and can be useful if a dog needs to gain some weight or be enticed to eat, and as bait for training exercises.

Home Cooking

Most of the commercial products on the market are the result of years of testing and scientific formulation. They are designed to be nutritionally complete and safe for all pets. If you prefer to prepare your own food, you must also take pains to prepare a mixture that fulfills all the dog's nutritional needs. Contact a veterinarian or nutritionist for guidelines on all dietary requirements.

Devising an individual blend of kibble, meat, vegetables, and supplements has been shown to be an effective way to lower the monthly food expense for the owners of one or more rottweilers. In addition, feeding a homemade diet can be the most effective way to attend to the special needs of the breed and your individual dog. For example, rottweilers involved in vigorous work may require a diet enhanced with extra meat, carbohydrates, and fats. Elderly dogs may need an easily digested formula, whereas overweight or inactive dogs will require a low-calorie diet. Growing puppies and pregnant or lactating bitches require a diet high in protein and calories.

Supplementation

Supplementation is often too much of a good thing. In most cases, a commercially prepared diet

Feeding Your Rottweiler

that has been shown to be "nutritionally complete" will keep your rottweiler in top condition, as long as a good dose of exercise also is included. Oversupplementation of an already balanced diet is a more common occurrence than malnutrition, and the end result can be skeletal diseases, neurological disorders, and temperament problems induced by chemical imbalances in the diet.

It is especially important not to oversupplement puppies, as this can cause serious side effects and interfere with the normal growing process. A nursing or pregnant bitch may at times require vitamin supplementation, but this need should be diagnosed by a professional and medication should be administered under veterinary supervision.

Many breeders believe that the modern rottweiler's diet is lacking in roughage, and they augment it by supplying the dog with a daily carrot, apple, or a few crunchy biscuits. Unless given in large amounts, such an addition will not affect the nutritional balance of the dog's diet. However, loading the dog's meal down with fatty meat scraps can have a noticeable effect and result in diarrhea. Small amounts of fruits, vegetables, and cereals can promote proper digestion.

Giving your rottweiler a hard or crunchy food, such as carrots or a sturdy knuckle bone, can help to keep the dog's teeth clean because it will scrape away some of the tartar that accumulates along the tooth surface. Care must be taken when choosing bones, however, because an inappropriate bone can splinter when chewed. Nylon or rawhide bones are the safest choice among the commercial products.

The Feeding Process

Rottweilers are enthusiastic eaters, and the owner will want to ensure that this is a controlled experience and a simple process. If handled properly, the daily meals should not overly excite the dog or cause it to growl protectively once given its meal.

A dog must be allowed to eat its meal in peace. It should not be rushed or made to feel nervous. An out-of-the-way place is most appropriate; expecting the dog to eat in the middle of the kitchen at the busiest time of day undoubtedly will cause the dog to constantly monitor the movement throughout the area and worry whether its food is going to be taken away. Bad habits, such as an aggressive attitude toward the food, can develop in response to the dog's anxiety. This habit cannot be tolerated. A rottweiler must be trained from an early age to allow its master to pick up and remove its food, if necessary, without protest. An anxious dog often will devour its food quickly, which can result in digestive problems or vomiting.

The dog's natural appetite and the amount of food it will consume will vary depending on its size, age, sex, metabolism, and activity level, as well as the quality of the diet. When trying to determine how much food your rottweiler will need daily, use the amount listed on the label as a guide. Working rottweilers naturally would require more calories each dog than an older, less active dog.

The age of the dog is the main factor in determining when to feed the dog each day. Puppies require four or five small meals a day, until approximately four to six months of age when they can be switched to three. At approximately nine to twelve months of age the meals can be reduced to only two daily. Rottweilers used as overnight guards often are fed only one large meal a day, given in the morning so that the dog is alert during the night.

The dog should be given ample time to eat its meal. Fifteen minutes usually is sufficient. Pick up and discard any food that remains after this time. If the dog is leaving food uneaten, decrease the amount slightly at the next meal and continue varying the amount until the dog clears its bowl. If the dog quickly empties its bowl, increase the amount slightly each meal until the dog is satisfied.

A sudden lack of interest in eating usually is

caused by a health or behavioral problem. If your dog refuses its food, discard it and do not offer a replacement until the next scheduled meal. If the problem persists for more than a few meals the dog should be examined by a veterinarian. If there is no physical reason for this lack of appetite, chalk it up to stubbornness. Few dogs will continue this for long once they see that you will not give in.

If the dog appears hungry but still turns away, try another quality food to see if the dog somehow developed an aversion to what you were feeding it. You should not change the diet more than once, however, as the dog may learn to enjoy having you cater to its tastes. Rottweilers rarely are problem eaters, however.

Chewing

Every puppy has the urge to chew when it is teething and shedding its first teeth, and again when its back molars are emerging. Many owners are fooled into thinking that chewing will then end, but in fact a dog will chew throughout its life. The amount of chewing will vary from dog to dog, and is affected by the dog's age, temperament, training, and level of exercise.

Chewing hard substances can be beneficial, as it helps remove some of the tartar buildup that has accumulated on the teeth. Because there is little of this in the regular diet, other objects must be found.

Many rottweilers like to chew, and find it a pleasurable pastime. Some rottweilers chew to release tension, often causing extensive and expensive damage to household goods. A rottweiler that is left alone for long stretches of time often placates its loneliness by chewing.

It is a pretty safe bet to say that every rottweiler will do some destructive chewing, especially from puppyhood through three years of age. Because there is no simple, foolproof method to stop chewing, the owner's best recourse to minimize the losses is to confine the dog whenever it cannot be

supervised and to always have a suitable chew toy available. Most rottweilers enjoy rawhide bones, but they usually can devour them in short order. This can become quite expensive, and may pose some health problems as large chunks of undigested rawhide can sometimes cause constipation or blockage. Nylon bones are long lasting and sturdy, but many dogs don't like them. Hard beef or veal bones, such as from the knuckle, should only be given occasionally, as they can be constipating and abrasive to the tooth enamel if the dog is an energetic chewer.

The owner must let the dog know exactly what *may* and *may not* be chewed upon. Be realistic: you cannot expect a dog to understand that it is okay to chew on an old slipper but not on the new pair. Never allow a puppy to chew on electric wires, as the resulting shock could prove fatal. Dogs must also be taught to stay away from household plants; many, like poinsettia or foxglove, are poisonous if ingested.

When you catch the dog with a forbidden object in its mouth, remove it from the dog's clutches, shake it in front of the dog's head and tap it as you say "No!" in a stern voice. Immediately give it something it is allowed to chew. In this way you will help the dog connect your displeasure with its chewing of the object. If the dog continues to chew, add a shake of the neck to your verbal correction and place the dog in a lengthy down-stay (see page 67).

Top: In show competition, your rottweiler will be judged ▶ as to how well it compares to the exacting requirements of the breed standard. Bottom: Rottweilers should exhibit a powerful trotting gait.

Grooming Your Rottweiler

Care of the Coat

The rottweiler has a coarse, dense outer coat that lies flat to its body, as well as an undercoat that must be present on the neck and thighs while not showing through the outer coat. The amount of undercoat is influenced by climatic conditions and seasonal changes and serves as a layer of insulation against the cold and heat.

Although all breeds go through a shedding period once or twice a year, the rottweiler does not lose excessive amounts of hair. The coat will have to be brushed once or twice a week with a medium to firm bristle brush or a hound glove (a grooming glove with short bristles in the palm that helps remove dead hairs). These routine brushings will remove dead hairs that cling to the coat, and in the process will clean the skin and the shafts of the living hair. The rottweiler is a natural breed and its coat is never to be cut or trimmed (although show dogs often have stray hairs around their feet tidied and their whiskers trimmed for competition).

The following are some helpful hints for cleaning the dog's coat should it become soiled with hard-to-remove substances:

Chewing gum: rub the gum with some peanut butter, leave it on for a few minutes, then ease the gum out of the coat using a wide-toothed comb.

Oil-based paint: let it harden, then scissor off the hair. Never use turpentine, kerosene, or other solvents near the skin.

Tar (on feet or between toes): carefully clip off as much affected hair as possible, then soak the area with vegetable oil. Let the oil remain for several hours, then shampoo.

Grease: dust the area with cornstarch, let it absorb for one hour, then brush it out, shampoo, and rinse.

◀ Top: The ideal rottweiler has a compact build that denotes great strength. Bottom: A rottweiler's topline should be firm and level. Its chest is broad, with well-sprung ribs.

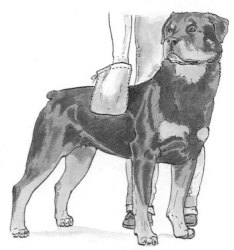

A rottweiler's coat is easily kept in good condition by the regular use of a hound's glove.

Odors: bathe the area in warm, sudsy water and rinse thoroughly. Pour a solution of vinegar and water over the dog and let it dry in. Repeat the process if necessary.

Bathing

The rottweiler should be bathed as infrequently as possible, usually only when the dog becomes excessively dirty or comes in contact with a foul substance. Given a proper dose of brushing, the rottweiler's coat should remain clean year-round and should give not give off a ''doggy'' odor.

When bathing is needed, use a very mild soap designed especially for dogs — not products for humans, which are too harsh and drying for a dog's coat. Wet the coat thoroughly, working the water down to the skin. Begin with the head and proceed down, being very careful that water and shampoo do not get into the dog's eyes and ears. Once the dog is fully lathered, rinse the coat well with lots of warm water. The soap must be totally removed from the undercoat or the skin may become irritated and the dog may develop dandruff. During cool weather you should towel dry the dog so that it is not exposed to any cold air until the undercoat is totally dry.

Care of the Nails

Rottweilers need a lot of outside exercise and activity, and through this most get enough exposure to rough pavement to keep the nails naturally worn down. During the weekly grooming session, owners should inspect their dog's nails to be sure they do not need to be trimmed, as overgrown nails can impede the normal placement of the foot and affect the dog's gait.

Few rottweilers enjoy having their feet held for any length of time. To counteract this natural reluctance and instinct to pull away, begin indoctrinating the puppy to having this area touched by regularly playing with its feet and toes while pet-

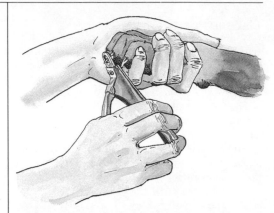

When nails need clipping, be sure to cut them on a slight angle, as shown. Remove only the outer shell of the nail; avoid the "quick," which will bleed if cut.

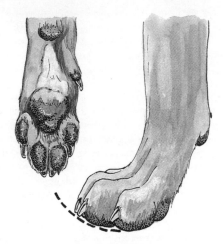

The rottweiler's foot is round and compact. To keep it in this condition, the nails must be kept short.

ting and grooming. You can later try massaging the footpads. This preparation will be valuable should the nails ever need to be clipped. If you are inexperienced, have your veterinarian show you this simple procedure at the dog's regular checkup. Once instructed, this process can be handled at home when required.

Use a specially designed "guillotine" clipper when trimming a dog's nails, not a product designed for humans. The proper equipment can be purchased from pet stores, grooming parlors, and veterinarians. Cut only the outer shell of the nail, as cutting too close to the vein (called the "quick") is quite painful for the dog and can cause bleeding. Once the nail is shortened to the proper length, smooth the surface with a few brushes of an emery board. Should you cut too close to the quick and the nail bleeds, apply pressure by holding a piece of cotton gauze over the nail or use a styptic pencil. Once the bleeding stops, dab the nail with a mild antiseptic.

If Your Rottweiler Gets Sick

The most successful method for safeguarding your pet's health is through monitoring the dog's outward appearance at home and backing this up with an annual physical examination by a veterinarian. He or she will evaluate the dog's general condition, test for internal parasites, and determine if the dog needs any injections. Through routine inspections such as these, you have a better chance of catching any potential health problems early, and cure rates are considerably higher when illnesses are caught in the beginning stages.

It also is vital that you bring your dog in for professional care if you notice such symptoms as weight loss or gain, drinking excessive amounts of water, lethargy, persistent vomiting or diarrhea, or change in the hair coat. A proper diagnosis by a veterinarian is essential because these symptoms can be associated with many disorders. Although most common illnesses are easily cured, many health problems can become life-threatening when left to "run their course" by slow-acting owners.

Evaluating Your Rottweiler's Health

A good way to keep close tabs on your rottweiler's outward condition is by performing a quick inspection of the dog during routine grooming sessions. Begin by running your hands over the dog's entire body and feeling for anything unusual, such as cuts, swelling, cysts, or areas that seem painful to the dog when touched. The rottweiler's dark coat may hide any visible signs of skin problems, so be sure to work your fingers down to the skin. You should then turn to the head and begin a more thorough evaluation.

Eyes

A healthy eye should be bright and shiny; it should not appear inflamed, bloodshot, or overly tear laden. The inner lining of the eyelid should be

The rottweiler's eye should be clear and free from discharge.

moist and pink, and the white of the eye should not show any yellowing. A slight discharge in the corner of the eyes is normal and can be cleared away easily with a damp, lint-free cloth. Do not use cotton balls, as this can leave tiny fibers behind in the eye. A clear discharge usually is related to the drainage of the tears and can be enhanced by minor irritations and inflammations such as conjunctivitis. Should this discharge become excessive or change color to cloudy or yellowish, or if the dog seems bothered by light, paws constantly at the eye, or blinks excessively and the eye is red, consult your veterinarian as an infection may be present.

It is not uncommon for a rottweiler to get a minor scratch on the eye while moving through the underbrush. This generally will heal on its own without requiring medical attention. Should a burr or small object get into the eye, immediately irrigate the eye with some warm water or carefully dab the corner of the eye with a soft cloth. Should a foreign object become lodged, seek immediate veterinary care, as probing for it may seriously injure the eye.

Ears

With pendant ears such as a rottweiler's, the owner will need to regularly check and clean inside every two weeks. A dog with ear problems constantly will shake its head or rub its ears with its paws or on the ground. If there is an excessive amount of visible earwax, redness, swelling, or a foul odor coming from the ear canal, a veterinarian's attention is required.

Never probe down into the dog's ear canal, as this can be extremely painful and can cause great damage. To help remove the normal buildup of wax and dirt in the outer ear, pull up the ear and swab the easily accessible areas with a cotton ball wet with a little warm water or with a wet cloth wrapped around your forefinger. Ointments made specially for cleaning the ear can be purchased from pet shops, grooming parlors, or your veteri-

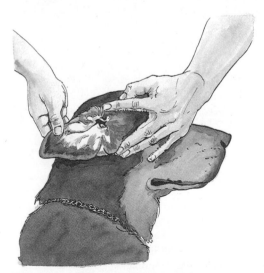

During the annual examination the veterinarian will inspect your dog's ear canal for any excessive buildup or signs of infection.

narian if cleanliness is a continual problem. Avoid oily compounds, as they may attract and retain dirt.

If you suspect that the inner ear is clogged with wax, bring the dog to your veterinarian for a thorough cleaning. If the problem is chronic, you can ask for instruction on how to perform this procedure at home.

Should the dog wince with pain when its ears are touched, an infection may be present. An inflammation of the ear, termed *otitis*, can be treated topically or with antibiotics. This condition can have several causes, such as parasitic mites or a bacterial or yeast infection. Large deposits of black or reddish-brown earwax commonly are found with ear disorders, and this discharge will have to be inspected microscopically to ensure an accurate diagnosis, so seek veterinary assistance at the onset of the problem.

Occasionally your rottweiler may get a minor abrasion on the ear flap. The most important task is to keep the afflicted area clean to avoid infection. Your veterinarian can advise you about what best to apply should you find a scratched or abrased area. Should you suspect that an object has somehow become lodged in the ear, seek immediate veterinary attention and *do not attempt to probe the ear yourself.*

Tooth Care

Few rottweilers eat a diet that contains enough natural abrasives to remove the tartar, or plaque, that builds up over the years at the gum line of the teeth. Although encouraging your dog to eat carrots and chew safe, hard bones will aid in tartar removal, this seldom is sufficient.

Unless conditioned, most adult dogs are reluctant to having their teeth cleaned, so you must accustom your rottweiler from puppyhood to allow you to gently clean its teeth with a soft child's toothbrush or a moistened gauze pad wrapped around your finger. A yellowing of the tooth exterior is common as the dog ages and often can be

If Your Rottweiler Gets Sick

minimized by routine treatment. The teeth can be brushed once or twice a week with a mild paste of baking soda and hydrogen peroxide to remove most stain and plaque. Special dental products designed for dogs also can be purchased from veterinarians or pet supply stores.

If discoloring remains despite weekly brushings, the teeth may need to be scaled by your veterinarian. If the buildup is chronic, your veterinarian can teach you how to perform this scaling at home as part of the dog's regular grooming process. Heavy deposits will need to be removed by ultrasonic scraping and the dog may need to be anesthetized if major cleaning is required.

Although cavities are seldom a problem for dogs, there are other conditions the owner should be aware of. A sudden change in the dog's breath that lasts for more than a few days may indicate a problem with either the teeth, tonsils, or throat. A loss of appetite could stem from tooth problems, as decayed teeth make it painful for the dog to eat. Inspect the teeth and gums for any obvious sign of infection, swelling, bleeding, or sensitivity to the touch. An abscessed tooth sometimes manifests itself as a boil-like growth on the cheek area. Your veterinarian should be informed as soon as you notice any of these conditions.

Feet

Working dogs, such as rottweilers, give their legs and feet a considerable pounding in the course of a normal day. Consequently, these areas are susceptible to various minor injuries. The pads of the feet should be inspected regularly and wiped with a clean, damp cloth whenever the dog is out in wet and cold weather. Should the dog limp or favor a leg, check the foot for burrs, splinters, chewing gum, or stones that may have become embedded in and between the pads of the foot. If necessary, use sterilized tweezers to carefully remove any object. Scratches and cuts on the pad are common. Nails can also be torn (see Care of the Nails, page 30). For minor problems, a gen-

tle cleaning with a mild antiseptic should be sufficient. An application of a little petroleum jelly often will soothe irritated feet.

A sudden limp or a furious case of licking the foot may indicate that the dog has been stung by an insect. Apply an ice compress to reduce or prevent swelling andease the pain. Unless the dog shows signs of an allergic reaction (see Stinging Insects, page 38), this discomfort should pass quickly.

If the dog indicates pain in the foot and there is no obvious cut or sting, then there may be an injury to the bones or muscle tissue or an object may be embedded deeply in the footpad. Hard at work or play, a rottweiler may turn too sharply and suffer a muscle pull. Although rarely serious, these conditions require the expertise of a veterinarian for a proper diagnosis.

The footpads require special attention during the winter months when your rottweiler's feet may be exposed to the chemicals that are placed on the sidewalks to melt ice and snow. These compounds can be caustic to a dog's feet and skin. If you suspect that your dog has walked on these chemicals, rinse its feet with warm, soapy water once it returns home. Follow this with a thin layer of petroleum jelly. If these irritating chemicals are not removed from the dog's feet it may try to lick them off. Ingesting such poisonous materials is extremely hazardous to the dog's digestive tract.

Basic Medical Procedures

A knowledgeable pet owner must be able to perform several simple procedures at home that will aid in assessing a pet's condition. Knowing how to take a pet's temperature and heart rate is vital when you suspect that your dog may be ill. By speedily performing these procedures you obtain some vital information about the animal's health—information that will be valuable for the veterinarian should the condition require emergency attention.

If Your Rottweiler Gets Sick

Taking the Temperature

As with humans, a dog often will respond to infection by running a fever. The owner must first be aware that a dog's normal temperature is slightly higher than a human's — 100.8° to 102.5° F (38.2°–39.2°C). To take a dog's temperature you must first lubricate the end of a heavy-duty rectal thermometer with a little petroleum or KY jelly. As a safety precaution, you may want to have an assistant help restrain the dog during the insertion and thereby prevent the dog from inadvertently sitting down or otherwise breaking the thermometer. It is best to have the dog stand on a table, but it can also lie on its side. One person should get a secure grasp on the dog while the other lifts the tail and inserts the thermometer. The thermometer should remain for one to two minutes to get an accurate reading.

Taking the Pulse

A dog's heartbeat and pulse also can be monitored easily. A rottweiler's heart normally beats from 60 to 100 times per minute while resting, but this rate may vary due to such factors as age, physical condition, external temperature, exertion, stress, and illness. To feel the heartbeat, you can place your fingertips against the dog's chest just behind its elbow, but this is less precise than taking a pulse rate. A pulse can be found in the front paw, but the one on the inside of the thigh near the groin is the easiest to locate. Press softly against the artery that is found there to find the pulse and monitor the pattern and rate of the beats. This procedure should be performed if you ever notice signs of extreme fatigue, fainting, or hyperactivity in your dog. Any abnormal patterns in the heartbeat require immediate attention by a veterinarian.

You also should be aware of your dog's normal breathing pattern. When relaxed, the breathing should be easy and smooth, from 10 to 30 breaths per minute.

Giving Medication

Giving your rottweiler a pill or capsule may seem like a simple enough procedure, but most dogs quickly master the technique for *not* swallowing pills and defiantly spit them right back out. The easiest method is to disguise the pill in something tasty, such as a small chunk of liverwurst, hamburger meat, or a piece of cheese that is swallowed quickly in one gulp. If your dog is not so easily tricked, gently pry the dog's mouth open by applying pressure at the back of its mouth, tilt the head up *slightly,* and insert the pill as far back on the tongue as possible. Close the jaws, give the dog a distracting pat, and watch for a swallow. Gently stroking the throat may encourage a reluctant dog to swallow. *Never lift a dog's head straight up and drop in a pill, as in this position the medicine can be inhaled into the windpipe rather than swallowed.*

The best way to administer liquid medicine is to place it in a medicine spoon or syringe and pour

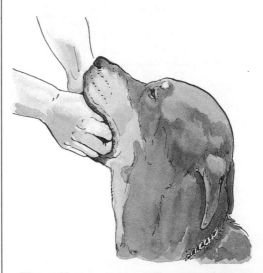

When giving your rottweiler a pill, apply gentle pressure at the back of the mouth to open it, tilt the head up slightly, and insert the pill at the back of the tongue.

If Your Rottweiler Gets Sick

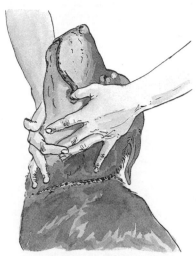

After inserting the pill, close the mouth and rub the neck to encourage the dog to swallow.

it into the *back of the mouth* by lifting up the side of the dog's lower lip by the back molars and holding the head *slightly* upward. This allows the medicine to slide down the throat. Keep a grasp around the dog's muzzle until you are sure it has swallowed, or the dog easily may spit the medicine out. Again, never hold the head in an exaggerated upward position, as this invites choking.

Some liquid and powdered medicines also may be mixed into the dog's food (check with your veterinarian first, however), but many dogs smell or taste the additives right away and will not eat the "tainted" food. If this is the case, powdered medications usually can be liquified by adding a little water, and you can proceed as described above.

Vaccinations

During the first few weeks of a puppy's life it receives antibodies from its mother that protect it from various diseases. Once weaned, however, the puppy becomes susceptible to communicable diseases and must be protected by receiving a series of vaccinations.

Most puppies receive their first immunizations at around five to six weeks of life, while they are still with their breeder. These include small dose vaccinations for canine distemper, infectious canine hepatitis, leptospirosis, and parvovirus. These first shots generally protect the dog for only a few weeks, so follow-up shots will be required for most vaccines, on a schedule devised by your veterinarian (generally at eight to ten weeks and again at twelve weeks). A rabies vaccination also will be needed at approximately three to six months of age, and most shots will require annual or biannual boosters as the dog matures to ensure continued protection.

By keeping current with the required vaccinations and boosters you can protect your dog from many of the infectious diseases that have proven to be killers. Through such medical advances diseases such as kennel cough, a respiratory disease that used to kill thousands of puppies each year, can be kept under control.

Be sure to request all records of your dog's earliest shots from the breeder and pass this information along to your veterinarian. Because worms are very common in puppies, you should also ask the breeder if the puppy has already been tested or treated for worms. If it has, find out what type of worm the puppy was infected with, what medication was used to treat it, and how the puppy reacted to the medication. This background information may prove very helpful for the veterinarian should the puppy become reinfested at some later date.

Internal and External Parasites

With outdoor-loving dogs such as a rottweiler, parasites are unfortunate facts of life. The owners' task is to keep a close watch on the dog's condition so that problems can be caught in the initial stages. This is important especially during the warmer months when infestations are more prevalent.

Worms

Worms are very common in dogs, especially puppies. Although infestations usually are cured easily with proper medication, they should never be ignored. Severe infestations can be very debilitating and sometimes life-threatening. Symptoms include weight loss, weakness, a bloated stomach, diarrhea, dull coat, and a poor or voracious appetite. The dog may drag its anus across the ground, or lick and bite around the tail area. Some infected dogs will give little outward sign of the problem until heavily infested, which highlights the importance of having the dog checked for worms at its annual checkup.

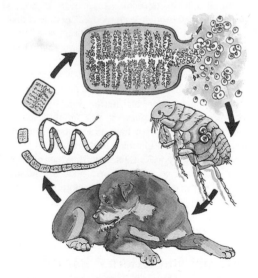

The life cycle of the adult tapeworm: Tapeworm eggs are ingested by fleas and hatch in the fleas' intestines. Should your rottweiler ingest an infected flea, the tapeworms will mature in the dog's intestines. Mature tapeworms in turn lay eggs that are passed in the dog's stool.

Detecting the presence of worms is done by microscopic examination of stool or blood samples. Only a veterinarian can properly diagnose the type of worm and select the proper medication. Well-meaning owners should never routinely worm a dog using over-the-counter preparations, as this process can be very dangerous and has led to numerous poisonings.

The most common types of worm are the roundworm, tapeworm, hookworm, and whipworm. Each requires a specific medicine that, in effect, poisons and kills the worms without hurting the dog.

Heartworm is another internal parasite that is spread primarily by mosquitos. Each year the dog must be given a blood test to determine whether it is free of the parasite. If no heartworms are present, a *preventive* medication can be administered on a monthly basis throughout mosquito season (early spring until after a killing frost) to keep the dog free from infection.

Fleas

Fleas are all but unavoidable during the warm months, especially if you and your dog enjoy walking through wooded areas (and what rottweiler doesn't!). Although this is a common problem, it shouldn't be underrated. Fleas can make a dog's life miserable. They invade the host, bite its skin, suck its blood, itch unbearably, and sometimes infect the dog with tapeworms. The severity of the problem usually depends on the local climate and the owner's diligence in detecting and ridding the fleas from the dog and its housing.

The rottweiler's dark coat can make detection difficult, so the owner must thoroughly and routinely inspect the dog's skin, especially if the dog is scratching or biting itself. Although you might not be able to pinpoint many of the swift-moving fleas, you easily can spot the small black and white feces and eggs they deposit in an afflicted dog's coat. Because the eggs are not attached to the dog's coat, they easily will fall off the dog and onto its bedding. They can also invade *your* carpeting, furniture, or bed. There, in eight to ten days, they will hatch into a new generation of pests.

For minor infestations, the fleas on the dog can be killed by using the powders and sprays designed especially for this purpose. They can be purchased at any pet store or grooming parlor. The coat must be doused thoroughly with the repellent in order for it to work, and the active ingredient must reach the skin. Be extremely careful when applying the material. *Read the instructions carefully.* Cover the dog's eyes, nose, mouth, and ears and slowly work the insecticide into the coat, working against the grain.

If the dog is heavily infested, a bath with a flea dip will be needed. Many grooming parlors supply this service, or you can do it at home. Always use products designed just for this purpose, and read all directions before beginning.

Once the dog has been cleared of fleas, you will have to make sure that the house, especially the dog's bedding, is also free of parasites and eggs. If the fleas have found their way into the household carpeting, a heavy-duty insect bomb (available at most hardware stores and pet shops) will be needed to destroy all the breeding colonies.

A flea collar will help protect the dog from reinfestation. Be sure to remove the collar should it get wet, as it can become irritating to the skin.

Ticks

Ticks are very painful for an afflicted dog, and can cause a variety of diseases, including anemia and paralysis. One variety of tick, the deer tick, can induce Lyme disease in dogs as well as other animals and humans. If left untreated, this disease leads to arthritis, severe headaches, and heart problems.

Although rather slow moving, ticks are not detected easily on rottweilers as they are merely a fraction of an inch when they enter the dog's coat. Although tick collars may help repel the parasite, they are only truly effective around the neck area. Infestations commonly can occur on the hindquarters and around the ears.

Once on a host, a tick's mouth gnaws through the dog's skin and the parasite is then implanted so that it can suck and live off the dog's blood. The tick will remain until it has drunk its fill, becoming engorged with the animal's blood and swelling to many times its normal size. At this point it will disengage itself, and may then lay a large quantity of eggs to perpetuate the cycle.

A tick must be removed carefully. If simply ripped from the skin, the tick's head can tear away from its body and remain embedded in the skin. This can result in an infection or abscess. Also, never try to burn a tick off your dog using a match or a cigarette. The dangers of this should be evident.

The proper way to remove a tick is to grasp it firmly, using a tweezer or your thumb and forefinger, as close to the skin as possible and apply firm but gentle upward pressure. *Do not twist.* An alternative method is to apply a tick dip, which can be purchased from most veterinarians or pet shops. This will, in effect, suffocate the tick and make it release its hold on the dog's skin. Once a tick has been removed, a small lump or swollen area may remain for several days.

Lice and Mites

Lice usually are spread through contact with another infested animal. Once on the dog, the lice deposit eggs that adhere to the dog's hair. Some diligence on the part of the owner may be required, as lice infestations often are difficult to cure.

Several types of mites infect different areas of the dog and produce a condition generally termed *mange.* Mites also can be transmitted to humans, so owners must treat afflicted animals quickly and effectively.

If Your Rottweiler Gets Sick

Although less common than flea and tick infestations, lice and mites can cause intense itching and uncontrollable scratching in afflicted dogs. This can cause extensive damage to the dog's coat and skin that may take a long time to heal, so it is important to catch skin problems in the early stages. If you notice any clusters of eggs, a rash of bumps, or pustules on the skin, consult your veterinarian for a proper diagnosis and treatment.

Stinging Insects

Luckily most insect bites are minor discomforts for a dog, just as for humans. Signs of a bite are difficult to detect, especially when occurring in the black parts of the rottweiler's coat. If you happen to witness your dog being bitten, or you notice a sudden onset of limping, check the site and see if a stinger is still embedded. If it is, carefully remove it by scraping your fingernail or the side of a credit card across the base of the bite using a scooping motion. This will remove the stinger and limit the spread of the venom. If possible, apply ice or a cold compress to the area to reduce swelling.

Occasionally a dog will have an allergic reaction to a bite. Reactions will vary from dog to dog, depending on its level of sensitivity and the amount of venom received. A case of hives or localized swelling generally will subside in a matter of hours, with no lasting effect. Administering an over-the-counter antihistamine (as advised by your veterinarian) or a corticosteroid will relieve most allergic reactions. A more severe reaction, such as marked swelling or difficulty in breathing, requires immediate veterinary attention.

If your dog has had an allergic reaction to stinging insects, consult with your veterinarian and devise a strategy for coping with future emergencies and have the antidotes readily available at all times.

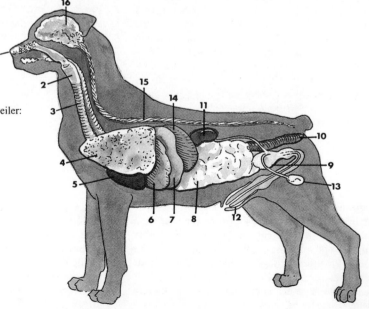

The internal organs of the rottweiler:
1. sinus cavity
2. thyroid cartilage
3. trachea
4. lungs
5. heart
6. liver
7. stomach
8. small intestine
9. bladder
10. rectum
11. kidneys
12. penis
13. testes
14. spleen
15. spinal column
16. brain

If Your Rottweiler Gets Sick

Common Illnesses

Throughout their lives, most dogs — just like humans — will contract a few minor illnesses. If handled properly, these disorders should pass quickly. However, because dogs are unable to verbally communicate their discomforts, it is up to the owner to accurately assess the dog's condition and decide whether veterinary attention is required.

Vomiting

Vomiting can have many causes. It is generally the result of a minor upset of the digestive tract. Most incidents will pass in a day or two and often are related to something the dog has eaten (such as grass, garbage, or paper) or to a virus that the dog has come in contact with. Severe, continued vomiting is very serious, however, and can lead to dehydration.

If the vomiting is limited to a few episodes, withhold all food for 12 to 24 hours. You can administer some Pepto-Bismol to help settle the dog's stomach and allow it to have a little water or some ice chips. If there is no sign of fever and the vomiting subsides, you can give the dog several small servings of easily digestible foods, such as kibble with a little scrambled egg or rice, over the next 24 hours. If the vomiting does not recur, the normal diet can be resumed the following day. Should vomiting continue or intensify, or if you should notice any blood or worms in the vomit, be sure to get the dog to a veterinarian at the very first opportunity.

Many dogs, especially the larger breeds such as the rottweiler, have a tendency to gulp their food. Because of a quick intake of air into the stomach, the dog suddenly may regurgitate the meal. The best solution for dogs prone to this is to serve several small meals each day rather than one or two large ones, thereby limiting the amount of food in the stomach at any one time. This eating pattern may be related to nervousness on the dog's part about its food. If this is the case, the owner must work with the animal to reassure it that there is nothing to fear. A dog such as the rottweiler must be responsive to its owner and must allow its meal to be removed, if necessary, without any aggressive or overly nervous reaction.

Diarrhea

As with vomiting, most cases of diarrhea are relatively mild. Diarrhea can result from contact with various viruses or bacteria, a change in the dog's diet or water supply, the dog eating something irritating or indigestible, or even an emotional upset.

Mild diarrhea usually can be treated at home, but should the condition worsen or continue for more than 24 hours, consult your veterinarian. Dehydration can occur quickly with persistent diarrhea. Immediate veterinary assistance is needed if you notice a bloody discharge or if the condition is combined with vomiting and/or a high fever. Bring a sample of the dog's stool for examination should veterinary help be required.

A mild case of diarrhea is treated by removing all food from the dog for the next 24 hours to allow the system to rid itself of any offending material in the intestinal tract. A small amount of water or ice cubes is permissible, however, as is a tablespoon of Kaopectate. If symptoms do not worsen during the next 24 hours, the dog can be allowed several small, bland meals containing a binding agent such as rice or oatmeal. If the condition does not recur, you can resume the normal diet in three days.

Constipation

If your dog does not move its bowels in its normal pattern, especially if this lasts for 48 hours, it may be suffering from constipation. Symptoms include listlessness and loss of appetite. Occasionally, a constipated dog may vomit.

Constipation is more common in older dogs or those that chew meat bones (the chips of which are indigesible and harden the stools). Constipation most often occurs when a dog undergoes a sudden change of diet. Confining a dog for too long a time may also cause this problem as the dog restrains its natural urges to eliminate until allowed outside. In such cases, the problem usually is temporary and can be alleviated by administering a mild laxative, such as milk of magnesia (ask your veterinarian for the proper dosage, based on your dog's weight).

If you have a dog that is prone to constipation, you should make an effort to add a little extra roughage or one tablespoon of mineral oil twice daily to the dog's normal diet to aid proper elimination. Should the condition linger, your veterinarian may suggest the use of a glycerine suppository or a warm water enema to alleviate the blockage.

Should you ever see the dog actively straining, crying out with pain, and not passing any excrement, seek professional care at once. The dog may have swallowed an object that is now lodged in the intestinal tract, causing a life-threatening situation. Alternatively, constipation can be caused by a tumor, an enlarged prostate gland, or a hernia that may be interfering with the normal functioning of the intestines. Such situations are emergencies that require specialized veterinary care.

Impacted Anal Glands

At the base of the dog's anus are two sacs that secrete a strong-smelling substance used by the dog as a scent marker. The anal sacs, sometimes referred to as the "stink glands," normally are emptied during the defecation process. If, however, they are not cleared completely by the normal elimination process they can become impacted and will require manual emptying.

The symptoms of impacted anal sacs include a constant licking of the area and/or dragging the anus across the ground or floor. (This also can be symptomatic of worm infestation.) If the anal sacs

appear full, they can be expressed manually by carefully pressing along the outsides and back of the sacs with your thumb and forefinger positioned on either side of the gland. Be sure to hold a tissue below the gland to collect the fluid that flows out. Have your veterinarian show you this procedure the first time, as proper technique is required so as not to hurt the dog. Should this procedure seem painful to the dog, or if there is any pus or blood mixed in with the fluid, an infection may be present that will require veterinary attention.

Hip Dysplasia

Hip dysplasia (HD) is a potentially crippling disease that can be found in rottweilers, as well as most of the medium and large breeds that undergo rapid growth early in life. HD is a malformation of the hip joint that produces an improper fit of the hip socket and the femur bone. Constant friction caused by movement in an afflicted hip slowly wears the joint down as the dog ages, ultimately leading to pain when walking or during sudden movement. The first clinical signs of the disease generally do not appear until the dog is five to eight months of age. Paralysis can occur in severely dysplastic dogs. Although steps can be taken to relieve the pain and slow the course of the disease, there is no cure.

Because HD primarily is hereditary, the best way to eliminate the problem is by breeding only those dogs that do not have a predisposition for the disease. When buying your rottweiler—especially if you intend on breeding—you should investigate not only the potential puppy, but the parents and grandparents as well for any sign of the disease. Every rottweiler intended for breeding should be x-rayed at approximately 12 to 15 months of age for signs of HD. The X-rays are then sent for evaluation by specialists from the Orthopedic Foundation for Animals (OFA) or by at least two board certified veterinary radiologists at a university veterinary school. Only those rott-

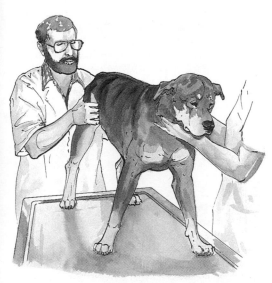

During the annual checkup, the veterinarian will closely examine your rottweiler's hindquarters for signs of hip dysplasia.

weilers certified as clear of the problem should be used in any breeding program.

Although genetics plays an important role in this disease, environmental factors also can affect its onset. Improper nutrition or overfeeding during the first year of life can increase the likelihood of HD in rottweilers.

Emergency Procedures

Injuries

Speed is the most important factor when you are dealing with an emergency situation. Should your dog sustain a serious injury, your first act must be to calm and restrain the dog so that it cannot move about and cause further damage to itself. Only then can you transport the dog to a veterinarian. Internal problems may be present that are not visible to the eye.

An injured dog is terrified and instinctively may lash out at anyone who comes near it, so approach the animal cautiously and protect yourself from being bitten. Speak to it in low, soothing tones. A stocking, tie, or thin piece of cloth can serve as an emergency muzzle. (You should never use a muzzle on a dog that has chest injuries or is having difficulty breathing, however.) Fold the material in half and place a knot at the midpoint. Make a second loop approximately 6 inches (15.2 cm) above the knot and place the dog's muzzle in the hole formed between the two. Pull the top loop tight over the muzzle, with the knot remaining under the jaw. Take the two ends and cross them under the jaw and around to the back of the head. Tie a secure knot, but be sure it is not too restrictive. You are now ready to attend to the dog.

Only move an injured animal when absolutely necessary, such as to remove it from a site where it may incur further damage. Inspect the skin and

An emergency muzzle can be made from a belt, tie, stocking, or thin piece of cloth. Place the center fold on top of the muzzle. Cross the two bands under the jaw and around the back of the head. Tie a secure knot, but do not make it so tight as to be painful for the dog.

locate the source of any bleeding. If possible, gently wash the area with soap and warm water. If the blood continues to flow, apply a clean cloth or gauze pad to the site, secure it if possible, and hold the compress in place until the bleeding stops. Unless the cut is very small, it will need professional attention. A veterinarian will be better able to apply a bandage that will stay in place.

If a bone appears to be broken, immobilize the dog to the best of your ability and get it to your veterinarian as quickly as possible. If allowed to move about, the dog may damage the muscles, tendons, cartilage, and nerves surrounding the break. Try to keep the dog calm. If necessary, you can use a blanket as a makeshift stretcher for transporting the dog short distances.

An injured dog quickly can go into shock, so cover it with a blanket for added warmth and monitor its heart rate. Never give an injured dog anything to eat or drink, especially alcohol. Knowing the dog's vital signs will be an aid for the veterinarian once help arrives. If the dog lapses into unconsciousness, check that its breathing passages are open. Get the dog onto its side. Gently pry open its mouth and pull the tongue forward to allow air to flow into the lungs.

Poisonings

Unfortunately, most accidental poisonings occur without the owner ever knowing that the dog has ingested a poisonous substance. This often has serious consequences as *immediate* action is required if the dog is to survive a poisoning. Symptoms of poisoning include diarrhea, vomiting, lethargy, muscle spasms, shaking, dizziness, and increased salivation.

If you suspect that your dog has been poisoned, immediately seek professional help. Do not begin treating the dog yourself. The local poison control center often can supply you with some advice, but your veterinarian should see the dog as quickly as possible.

If you know the cause of the poisoning, and have the packaging, some information on the proper antidote may be supplied on the container. It will aid your veterinarian greatly to know how much poison was ingested and when in order to formulate the proper method for getting it out of the dog's system. Various procedures are used, depending on what type of poison has been ingested. Sometimes the stomach is pumped, sometimes the poison is neutralized.

Many well-meaning owners have been the cause of poisonings by administering excessive amounts of over-the-counter worming products and flea and tick preparations. Because household items are the most common sources of poisoning (not only for house pets but also for children), owners must keep all cleaning agents, pesticides, medicines, and painting supplies locked up. Items stored in a garage or shed should be kept at a height that the dog cannot reach and must be secured carefully to avoid spills. Antifreeze particularly is dangerous for dogs. It has a pleasant odor and taste that attracts the dog to it, but the ingestion of even a tiny amount can cause severe kidney damage.

Never allow your dog to chew on plants because many plants found in the house and garden are poisonous if ingested. The most common poisonous plants are philodendron, poinsettia, and daffodil bulbs.

Caring for Your Rottweiler as It Ages

Routine examinations of your rottweiler as it ages provide your veterinarian with the opportunity to be familiar with your dog while in its prime. This, in turn, enables him or her to better diagnose and catch problems that may arise while they are in their early stages. Such good basic care often results in a longer, healthier life for your dog.

A well-cared-for rottweiler should remain vig-

If Your Rottweiler Gets Sick

orous and healthy for many years. Even if your rottweiler has been spared the problem of hip dysplasia throughout its life, it may develop a general joint stiffness as it ages. Arthritis is common for many dogs, and can be aggravated in overweight dogs or ones that have been very physically active throughout their life. Owners of such dogs should discourage the dog from climbing stairs whenever possible (you may have to move its bed from its old spot upstairs to a more accessible spot on the first floor, for example) and should not engage the dog in games that will require sudden turns or jumps.

As a dog ages its digestive system may be the first to give the dog problems. Constipation is common in elderly dogs (often due to prostate problems), but changes in the dog's diet often can help alleviate this. During the dog's yearly checkup, ask your veterinarian whether a dietary change is in order for your dog. There are several quality diets on the market designed especially for older dogs. Most elderly dogs are placed on a diet that contains easily digested meats (such as poultry or fish). Your veterinarian may also suggest that you add several teaspoons of supplemental mineral oil or bran to its daily meal and may prescribe vitamin supplements, should the dog appear run down.

The owner must be sure there is always an adequate supply of clean water available.

Many elderly rottweilers slowly lose weight. This can result from several causes. Should you spot a weight loss, be sure to have the dog checked by your veterinarian to rule out any life-threatening condition. (For example, weight loss has been associated with a degeneration of the ability of the liver and kidneys to properly manage waste materials.) In many cases, adding a little extra fat to the diet will help elderly dogs retain their weight.

When tartar has been allowed to accumulate on a dog's teeth throughout its life the end result often is dental problems in elderly dogs. The elderly dog may have sensitive teeth, and this inevitably will cause it to stop the heavy chewing that removes tartar. Bad breath is common. A weekly brushing of the teeth can minimize this, but plaque removal by your veterinarian often is required. Dogs with heavy plaque buildup can develop systemwide health problems that stem from bacteria entering the system through the problem teeth and gums. Dental care often is regarded as a low priority by many pet owners, but the consequences of poor dental hygiene can be quite devastating.

Understanding the Rottweiler

Today's rottweilers, as well as all modern breeds, trace their roots back many thousands of years to the wolf-like dogs that once roamed the earth with the early ancestors of man. One popular theory on how the human-dog bond began posits that the dog initially was drawn to man in search of scraps from the hunt and the warmth of the cooking fire. Humans were, in turn, drawn to the dogs as aids in the hunt and guardians of the community.

Man valued the dogs' well-developed senses and physical prowess, and recognized that some were better suited to working and living with humans than others. Those with agreeable dispositions and superior abilities were selected for breeding; those that were vicious or fearful probably were eaten. Life was harsh, and food was limited.

These early dogs already exhibited a well-established hierarchy. The most assertive dog was the leader of the pack, and the other pack members fell in somewhere along the pecking order behind the leader.

Man was quick to learn that if the puppies were raised within the human family and handled when young, they adapted more fully to having *man* as the leader of the pack. This close interaction not only bonded the dog to humans, but the humans learned that dogs could be more than just workers — they also were fine companions. The human-dog bond was formed, and it continues to this day.

History of the Rottweiler Breed

The modern rottweiler is believed to have descended from the powerful draft dogs that were brought to southern Germany nearly 2,000 years ago by the conquering Roman armies. These early mastiff-type dogs were used to haul the supply carts and guard the camp, and they were valued for their willingness to work, great intelligence, and strong guarding instinct. Over time they interbred with the local herding dogs and through the generations a new breed evolved.

The breed traces its name to the town of Rottweil, a cultural and trade center that in the twelfth century was a center for the cattle industry and had a high concentration of butchers. The dogs commonly were used to drive cattle to and from the markets and they became known as "butcher dogs."

These early rottweilers flourished until the middle of the nineteenth century, when better roads and transportation methods led to many changes. Driving cattle was outlawed, and the dog cart soon was replaced by the railroad. With no work for the dogs to perform, their numbers plummeted. The breed was in danger of extinction, but several German breeders devoted to this tireless worker kept breeding them through the years, striving to preserve the original breed type. At the beginning of the twentieth century, the rottweiler was discovered to be an exceptional police and army dog, and the breed once again began to increase in numbers.

The rottweiler breed first was introduced in the United States around 1910 and slowly increased in number until there were enough dogs to be accepted for registration by the American Kennel Club on April 9, 1935. The breed numbers showed a slow, steady increase until the 1970s when "guard" dogs became vogue. The Doberman pinscher was the first of the working breeds to skyrocket in popularity, with the rottweiler following several years behind. During the 1980s the rottweiler eclipsed the Doberman in popularity and is now the most popular of the working breeds, with registrations that top other Working Group members by more than two to one.

These well-trained rottweilers perform extended sit and down-stays for their master. Such exemplary dogs reflect the owner's dedication to thorough training, as well as the dogs' desire to please their master. ▶

Understanding the Rottweiler

Behavior Patterns

The progenitors of today's dogs were shaped over the generations by selective breeding. Primitive man chose dogs whose traits most fit his needs, and as those needs changed he introduced other bloodlines. Centuries later many distinctive breeds had emerged, fulfilling the needs of various owners in various terrains. The characteristics and traits that man found most useful survived, whereas others were carefully bred out.

Some basic instincts have survived through the years, including pack behavior. When a group of unfamiliar dogs are placed together they instinctively will establish a hierarchy for this new pack. They will inspect each other's anal area. The most dominant dogs immediately will vie for the leadership. They will snarl, stand well up on their feet, and try to intimidate the opponent. Fierce growling and a fight may break out, but the weaker animal usually will yield quickly to the more dominant dog. The emerging leader is the "alpha" dog.

The domesticated dog has been asked to adapt to the rules of the human pack, but maneuvering for power still takes place — this time between dog and master. If the human does not exhibit what the dog perceives as leadership qualities, it feels entitled to vie for leader.

This "leader-of-the-pack" instinct is particularly keen in rottweilers, and often becomes pronounced during puberty. Owners must exhibit an assertive, consistent manner when dealing with the dog. In addition, the dog must understand that it is subordinate to *all* humans in its pack, not only a primary master. It is unwise to encourage the rottweiler to become a one-man dog. Rottweilers frequently bond most closely to one member of the home, but they must obey all. Obedience instruction should begin as soon as the puppy is introduced into the household, and all members must be shown the proper procedure for controlling the dog. Your rottweiler already has been indoctrinated by its dam, the original alpha, so with firm, consistent guidance it should learn quickly to accept its assigned place as pet — not leader — of the home.

Verbal and Nonverbal Communication

Even among distinct breeds, there are common forms of expression. Methods of nonverbal communication, such as facial expression, vocalization, and body language, basically are the same among all types of dogs and form their frame of reference. Dogs are adept at interpreting nonverbal cues. Subtle differences in sounds and movements have significance, and a dog's responses are influenced by the signals it receives.

A dog will react not only to verbal commands, but also to the master's vocal tones and physical demeanor. What an owner says often is not reflected in what his or her body language is showing, and the dog gets mixed messages. What the dog is feeling is expressed in its body language, and better communication will result if owners learn the meaning of their dog's various forms of posturing.

Because the rottweiler's tail normally is docked close to its body, this valuable "mood indicator" is more limited in this breed than with an undocked breed. However, even a stub can give you an idea of how the dog is feeling.

When relaxed, a rottweiler's ears are back somewhat, its muscles are at ease, and its weight appears evenly distributed. When happy, its ears are up, and it may whine or give off some short barks. When inviting play it will often drop its front to the ground while keeping its hindquarters

◀ Top, left: This rottweiler enjoys an outing in the park. When the owner stops to rest for a moment, the dog sits quietly in front of her. Top, right: This rottweiler patiently awaits release from a sit-stay. Bottom: It is important to train your rottweiler to heel when walking.

up (and its tail will be moving). When alert, the ears are pulled forward, there may be some wrinkling on the forehead, the tail is carried slightly above horizontal, its muscles appear rigid, and the dog is standing up on its toes.

An aggressive rottweiler will have an angry expression, its flews raised, its ears pulled forward, and it may bare its teeth and emit low growls. A fearful dog does not look as menacing as an aggressive dog, but it is unpredictable and therefore quite dangerous. Its face is slightly tensed, the ears pulled against the head, and the overall body position is lowered. If the dog feels threatened, it quickly can lunge at the perceived attacker from this position.

A timid or submissive dog assumes a lowered position with ears pulled slightly back, and its fur appears raised. It will avoid eye contact, and its eyes look rolled down and whiter than usual. Humans sometimes misinterpret this as the dog acting "guilty"; it is, in fact, yielding itself to a more dominant authority. A submissive dog also may attempt to lick the mouth or hands of the dominant individual. It may roll onto its back or even urinate. A confused dog also may assume a lowered stance, but it will not grovel or try to lick. Instead, it may pant rapidly, which is indicative of stress.

Communicating with Your Rottweiler

Regardless of the impression its size and build may impart to the eye, the rottweiler is a sensitive dog. It is not a brute and should never be treated as one. The best way to encourage a rottweiler to learn and retain information is through positive reinforcement, not through harsh techniques.

Praise, patience, and consistency are a trainer's most effective tools. To be an effective leader you must clearly show the dog what it is expected to do, and praise it highly when the task is accomplished. When mistakes are made, the dog should be corrected promptly and then once again shown the proper action. When the action is finally completed, the dog should then be praised for its good work. Mistakes are forgotten.

Every rottweiler is different, as is every trainer. Each individual has its own set of strengths and weaknesses that it brings to the learning process. The well-bred rottweiler is a capable learner, although some may be more stubborn or easily bored by training procedures than others. Some owners are better trainers than others. Both dog and owner will need to adapt and work out a system that works for them, and this involves trial and error.

When training a rottweiler, an owner will have to contend with the dog's pronounced protective instincts. This is a responsibility that cannot be ignored, as the dog instinctively will dislike having strangers approach its master. The dog will need to be taught restraint and to accept "outsiders." In addition, the owner has a responsibility to protect strangers from the dog and never place them in a situation where they suddenly are confronted alone by the dog. Although a rottweiler rarely will bite without provocation, it can easily intimidate the unwary visitor.

Training and handling the rottweiler can take skill, and novices should seek out an experienced professional as soon as they encounter problems. In homes where the dog is to be primarily a companion, select a trainer that previously has worked with rottweilers, and whose expertise includes more than just the "protection" aspect of this breed. Not all rottweilers are suited for Schutzhund-type work, and not all owners want to cultivate this side of the dog. Select a trainer that is assertive, but avoid the overly rough trainer. Every well-bred rottweiler wants to please its master, and it does not have to be physically manhandled to be taught obedience.

Good communication between a rottweiler and its owner requires more than a heavy hand. It is a commitment based on sensitivity, patience, and time.

Understanding the Rottweiler

Living with a Rottweiler

No master could ask for a more loyal, loving companion than a rottweiler. With those they love, they are openly affectionate and fun-loving. With those they don't know, they are aloof and wary. Their size and strength make them special, and special pets require special owners. The owners should be active and they should include the dog in as many activities as possible. The rottweiler is not for everyone, but a well-socialized rottweiler can be a trusted family member and a loving friend.

A rottweiler requires supervision. Its exercise requirements are substantial during the first few years of its life, but decrease a bit as an adult. A rottweiler is slow to mature, and may take not reach full "bloom"—both physically and mentally—until three years of age. Its grooming requirements are minimal, as it naturally is clean and odorless, and the normal life expectancy is nine to eleven years.

This breed's use as a watchdog is legendary, and this natural guardian instinct insures that the breed desires to remain near its home and loved ones. It seldom will roam.

A rottweiler is a fearless dog with a high tolerance for pain. An overly aggressive dog could be a danger to all around it, so much care must be taken in the selection and training of a puppy to ensure that it will develop into a calm, controlled adult. Overly rough play, tag games, and teasing should always be avoided, as overstimulation of the dog can result.

Companionship is vital in a rottweiler's life. It will not do well without plenty of human attention. When allowed to work with its master, the rottweiler gives wholeheartedly to whatever task it is presented.

The Working Rottweiler

The rottweiler breed was brought back from the verge of extinction because of its working ability. It excelled as a police and army dog. Its intelligence and loyalty proved steadfast no matter what the danger or duty. Today the rottweiler is the breed of choice for those looking for a guardian, and this attests to the well-rounded personality and trainability of these dogs.

Owners of this breed will find that rottweilers excel in many sports and types of competition. Show-quality rottweilers are among the most popular entries at conformation shows. For training enthusiasts, rottweilers take naturally to obedience competition. There are training clubs dedicated strictly to this sport, and obedience trials routinely are held in conjunction with most large AKC conformation shows.

Schutzhund competition originated in Germany but has become in recent years a major sport among American rottweiler enthusiasts as well. The training is rigorous. Schutzhund dogs are required to master a combination of advanced obedience, tracking, and protection skills. Only dogs with stable temperaments and well-developed protection instincts can excel in this sport, where control and drive are of utmost importance.

The rottweiler also is becoming a top competitor in weight-pulling competitions. This utilizes the breed's natural power and strength, and reflects the rottweiler's heritage as a cart dog. There are several types of competition, including sled or cart pulling, in which the dog is harnessed and challenged to pull loads of various weights. Competitors in this sport must be extremely well conditioned, and many began by enthusiastically pulling the children in their household on daily jaunts in the family wagon.

One of the most fulfilling activities a rottweiler can engage in is therapy work. Research has proven that animals enrich the lives of humans in ways that can reduce stress and make them happier and healthier. Organizations throughout the world, such as Therapy Dogs International or the Delta Society, currently are engaged in developing programs in which well-trained dogs visit elderly, sick, or emotionally disturbed people, as well as prisoners. The dogs are therapeutic aids that can help people in many ways — as aids for those struggling to recover from debilitating illnesses, such as a stroke, or as loving enticements for withdrawn and uncommunicative children. This pet-facilitated therapy has proven to be highly successful, and the cost is usually just a matter of a few hours time.

A German-born rottweiler named Ch. Mirko vom Steinkopf, CDX, was not only an international champion with obedience, tracking, and Schutzhund titles, but also a regular visitor to juvenile cancer patients undergoing treatment at a local hospital. He was reknown for nuzzling the patients and distracting them from their physical problems. Many parents praised the dog for help-

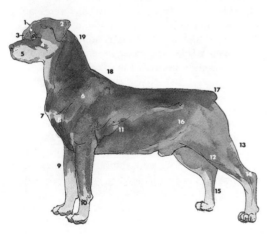

The anatomy of the rottweiler:

1. skull	11. ribcage
2. ears	12. stifle
3. stop	13. hindquarters
4. cheek	14. hock
5. muzzle	15. rear pastern
6. shoulder	16. loin
7. chest	17. tail
8. brisket	18. withers
9. forequarters	19. neckline
10. front pastern	

ing their children recover from their illness. Such a legacy lives on forever.

The Quality Rottweiler

The well-bred rottweiler is a robust and powerful dog. Males range from 24 to 27 inches (61–68.6 cm) in height at the shoulder, and 95 to 135 pounds (43.1–61.2 kg) in weight. Females are slightly smaller, ranging from 22 to 25 inches (55.9–63.5 cm) and 80 to 100 pounds (36.3–45.4 kg). Its power is even greater than its size.

The coat is always a glossy black, marked with a range of shades from tan or light brown to mahogany (with the darker shades more desirable). The markings are located as spots over each eye, on the cheeks and throat, a triangular mark on either side of the breastbone, under the tail, and at the base of the front and rear legs.

Rottweiler Standards

The official U.S. breed standard for the rottweiler, as devised by the American Rottweiler Club (the national breed club) and accepted by the American Kennel Club, and the international standard for the breed are listed below. These standards define the "ideal" rottweiler and serve as guides for judging the dogs in show competition. The details in the standards also are goals that dedicated breeders strive to produce in their dogs.

The AKC Rottweiler Standard

General Appearance

The ideal rottweiler is a medium large, robust, and powerful dog, black with clearly defined rust markings. His compact and substantial build denotes great strength, agility, and endurance. Dogs are characteristically more massive throughout with larger frame and heavier bone than bitches. Bitches are distinctly feminine, but without weakness of substance or structure.

Understanding the Rottweiler

Size, Proportion, and Substance

Dogs—24 to 27 inches (61–68.6 cm). Bitches—22 to 25 inches (55.9–63.5 cm) with preferred size being mid-range of each sex. Correct proportion is of primary importance, as long as size is within the standard's range.

The length of body, from prosternum to the rear-most projection of the rump, is slightly longer than the height of the dog at the withers, the most desirable proportion of height to length being 9 to 10. The rottweiler is neither coarse nor shelly. Depth of chest is approximately 50 percent of the height of the dog. His bone and muscle mass must be sufficient to balance his frame, giving a compact and very powerful appearance. *Serious Faults*—Lack of proportion, undersized, oversized; reversal of sex characteristics (bitchy dogs, doggy bitches).

Head

Of medium length, broad between the ears; forehead line seen in profile is moderately arched; zygomatic arch and stop well developed with strong, broad upper and lower jaws. The desired ratio of skull to muzzle is 3 to 2. Forehead is preferred dry, however some wrinkling may occur

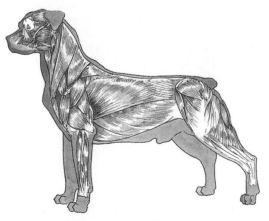

The musculature of the rottweiler.

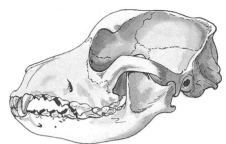

The skull of the rottweiler.

when dog is alert. Expression is noble, alert, and self-assured.

Eyes

Eyes of medium size, almond shaped with well-fitting lids, moderately deep set neither protruding nor receding. The desired color is a uniform dark brown. *Serious Faults*—Yellow (bird of prey) eyes; eyes of different color or size; hairless eye rim.

Ears

Ears of medium size, pendant, triangular in shape; when carried alertly the ears are level with the top of the skull and appear to broaden it. Ears are to be set well apart, hanging forward with the inner edge lying tightly against the head and terminating at approximately mid-cheek. *Serious Faults*—Improper carriage (creased, folded, or held away from cheek/head).

Muzzle

Bridge is straight, broad at base with slight tapering towards tip. The end of the muzzle is broad with well-developed chin. Nose is large and always black.

Lips

Always black; corners closed; inner mouth pigment is preferred dark. *Serious Fault*—Total lack of mouth pigment (pink mouth).

Understanding the Rottweiler

Bite and Dentition

Teeth 42 in number (20 upper, 22 lower), strong, correctly placed, meeting in a scissors bite — lower incisors touching inside of upper incisors. *Serious Faults* — Level bite, any missing tooth. *Disqualifications* — Overshot, undershot (when incisors do not touch or mesh); wry mouth; 2 or more missing teeth.

Neck, Topline, and Body

Neck is powerful, well muscled, moderately long, slightly arched and without loose skin. The back is firm and level, extending in a straight line from behind the withers to the croup. The back remains horizontal to the ground both while moving and standing.

The chest is roomy, broad and deep, reaching to elbow, with well-pronounced forechest and well-sprung, oval ribs. Back is straight and strong. Loin is short, deep, and well muscled. Croup is broad, of medium length and only slightly sloping. Underline of mature rottweiler has no distinct tuck-up.

Males must have two normal testicles, properly descended into the scrotum. *Disqualifications* — Unilateral cryptorchid or cryptorchid males.

Tail

Tail docked short, close to body. The set of the tail is more important than length. Properly set, it gives an impression of elongation of topline; carried slightly above horizontal when excited or moving.

Forequarters

Shoulder blade is long and well laid-back. Upper arm equal in length to shoulder blade, set so elbows are well under body. Distance from withers to elbow and elbow to ground is equal. Legs are strongly developed with straight, heavy bone, not set close together. Pasterns are strong, springy, and almost perpendicular to ground. *Feet* are round, compact with well-arched toes, turning neither in nor out. *Pads* are thick and hard; *nails* short, strong, and black. *Dewclaws* may be removed.

Hindquarters

Angulation of hindquarters balances that of forequarters. *Upper thigh* is fairy long, very broad, and well muscled. *Stifle* joint is well turned. *Lower thigh* is long, broad, and powerful, with extensive muscling leading into a strong hock joint. *Rear pasterns* are relatively short in length and nearly perpendicular to the ground. Viewed from the rear, hindlegs are straight, strong, and wide enough apart to fit with a properly built body. *Feet* are somewhat longer than front feet, turning neither in nor out, equally compact with well-arched toes. *Pads* are thick and hard; *nails* short, strong, and black. *Dewclaws* must be removed.

Coat

Outer coat is straight, coarse, dense, of medium length and lying flat. Undercoat must be

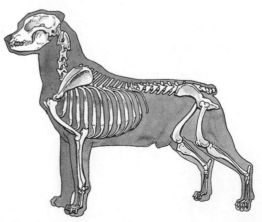

The skeleton of the rottweiler.

present on neck and thighs, but is not to show through outer coat. Amount of undercoat is influenced by climatic conditions. The coat is shortest on head, ears, and legs, longest on breeching. The rottweiler is to be exhibited in a natural condition with no trimming. *Fault* — Wavy coat. *Serious Faults* — Open, excessively short, or curly coat; total lack of undercoat; any trimming that alters the length of the natural coat. *Disqualification* — Long coat.

Color

Always black with rust to mahogany markings. The demarcation between black and rust is to be clearly defined. The markings should be located as follows: a spot over each eye; on cheeks; as a strip around each side of muzzle, but not on the bridge of the nose; on throat; triangular mark on either side of prosternum; on forelegs from carpus downward to toes; on inside of rear legs showing down the front of stifle and broadening out to front of rear legs from hock to toes, but not completely eliminating black from back of rear pasterns; under tail; black penciling on toes. The undercoat is gray or black. Quantity and location of rust markings is important and should not exceed 10 percent of body color. *Serious Faults* — Straw colored, excessive, insufficient, or sooty markings; rust marking other than described above; white marking any place on dog (a few rust or white hairs do not constitute a marking). *Disqualifications* — Any base color other than black; absence of all markings.

Gait

The rottweiler is a trotter. His movement should be balanced, harmonious, sure, powerful, and unhindered, with strong fore-reach and a powerful rear drive. The motion is effortless, efficient, and ground covering. Front and rear legs are thrown neither in nor out, as the imprint of hind feet should touch that of forefeet. In a trot the forequarters and hindquarters are mutually coordinated while the back remains level, firm, and rel-

atively motionless. As speed increases the legs will converge under body towards a center line.

Temperament

The rottweiler basically is a calm, confident, and courageous dog with a self-assured aloofness that does not lend itself to immediate and indiscriminate friendships. A rottweiler is self-confident and responds quietly and with a wait-and-see attitude to influences in his environment. He has an inherent desire to protect home and family, and is an intelligent dog of extreme hardness and adaptability with a strong willingness to work, making him especially suited as a companion, guardian, and general all-purpose dog.

The behavior of the rottweiler in the show ring should be controlled, willing, and adaptable, trained to submit to examination of mouth, testicles, and so on. An aloof or reserved dog should not be penalized, as this reflects the accepted character of the breed. An aggressive or belligerent attitude towards other dogs should not be faulted.

A judge shall excuse from the ring any shy rottweiler. A dog shall be judged fundamentally shy if, refusing to stand for examination, it shrinks away from the judge.

A dog that in the opinion of the judge menaces or threatens him or her, or exhibits any sign that it may not be safely approached or examined by the judge in the normal manner, shall be excused from the ring. A dog that in the opinion of the judge attacks any person in the ring shall be disqualified.

Summary

Faults — The foregoing is a description of the ideal rottweiler. Any structural fault that detracts from the above described working dog must be penalized to the extent of the deviation. *Disqualifications* — Overshot or undershot (where incisors do not touch or mesh); markedly wry mouth; 2 or more missing teeth; long coat; any base color other than black; absence of all markings.

Training Your Rottweiler

Rottweilers are the canine embodiment of size and strength. They have excelled in the role of guard and companion, exhibiting superlative natural protective instincts. These noteworthy trademarks of the breed require special handling if we are to produce dogs that are controlled and responsive to the wishes of the owner.

Inherent in dog ownership is a responsibility to properly train a pet so that it will exist peaceably and reliably with humans. The owners of a rottweiler have more than the average pet owner's responsibility — both moral and legal — to thoroughly train their dogs. Rottweilers are special dogs, requiring special owners. They must be available to carefully supervise the dog and capable of maintaining complete control of the animal at all times.

Modern day dogs retain instincts that trace back to their beginnings as pack animals, and this pack instinct affects the training process. The pack contains a hierarchy, and the most dominant — or "alpha" — member controls the pack and the others fall in line behind. The alpha position is one of respect. To obtain control over a pack animal an owner must earn the alpha position over his or her dog and, in effect, become leader-of-the-pack.

A puppy is exposed to its first doses of discipline shortly after birth. The dam is the indisputable leader of the litter — her pack — and she keeps her young in line. When the puppies assert their independence (as inquisitive rottweiler puppies will), the dam reprimands them using growls, a swat of the paw, or an occasional shake of the neck. Little else is needed. She admonishes her young swiftly, fairly, consistently, and unemotionally. These are the actions of a leader, and puppies learn to respect the wishes of the leader and to want to please him or her.

Owners should build on the basic disciplinary framework the dam has constructed and learn to correct and instruct their pets in a manner the dogs can understand. Should the dog misbehave, the owner must respond appropriately and consistent-ly. Even minor infractions must be corrected or this apparent lack of leadership will undermine the owner's alpha position and encourage the dog to misbehave again.

It is common for inexperienced trainers to react too harshly when training a rottweiler, given the breed's size and strength. As with any breed, the rottweiler responds well to positive training methods. Although a strong physical correction may sometimes be needed when the dog is being overly stubborn, the rottweiler does not need rough treatment to make it respond.

A good owner corrects firmly but fairly every time the dog misbehaves, letting it know what behavior is correct and what will not be tolerated. Brute force is not required and is counterproductive. The rottweiler is an intelligent, sensitive animal that wants to please its owner. Although a dog undoubtedly will test its owner's authority from time to time, there is no need to crush the dog's spirit through rough handling and physical abuse. Correct it in a manner a dog will understand — a firm vocal reprimand, a stern look, a shake of the neck. The dog already should understand the method and the meaning. Be sure never to whine, nag, plead, or preach at the dog, as these are not the actions of a leader. Strong physical corrections will be needed at times, but on the whole rottweilers will respond to conventional training methods taught with consistency, time, and patience.

Obedience is based on respect. If the dog does not respect you, it will not obey (unless out of fear, which is the worst possible case for a breed such as a rottweiler because a fearful dog is unpredictable). To earn the dog's respect, the owner uses abundant praise in response to good actions and clear corrections in response to misdeeds.

Rules for the Trainer

Lessons in basic house manners can begin from the time the dog first enters the home. If there is furniture that you do not want the adult dog to sit on, do not let the puppy sit on it either.

Training Your Rottweiler

Habits learned during the first days in the home are deeply ingrained, so be sure to monitor the puppy's actions. Gently but firmly correct misdeeds with a firm "No!" to show it what is unacceptable, but don't forget to enthusiastically praise the puppy when it does things right.

Getting a puppy to respond to its name is an important early lesson. This is accomplished easily by simply using the dog's name whenever you want it to come and lavishly praising the puppy when it responds. The dog will love the attention it is getting and subconsciously will learn how you look and react (verbally and nonverbally) when you, too, are pleased. This is the puppy's first success and it discovers that a correct response brings rewards. Positive reinforcement is the most effective method for making a puppy want to please you and this paves the way for a positive attitude about training. A rottweiler's desire to please its master should form the backbone of a training program and must always be fostered.

Formal training cannot begin until the puppy is capable of truly understanding what you want of it. Most rottweilers can begin learning the basic obedience commands at approximately six to eight months of age. Concentration is the key. If the puppy wanders off — either physically or mentally — it probably is too young for formal training lessons.

The initial lessons should be limited to no more than ten minutes, but they should be held two or three times each day. Repeat each lesson frequently, but stop as soon as the dog loses interest. Boredom seriously can damage a training program, and a bored rottweiler often will react by stubbornly refusing to obey.

The atmosphere should be pleasant, but serious. To encourage the dog to perform well for you, praise each minor success with "Good, General," and some pats. Don't get overly exuberant, however, or the dog will get so excited that it forgets what it is supposed to be doing.

Your tone of voice is very important when issuing commands. The command should be firm and authoritative, and be careful not to sound as if you are continually scolding the dog or, even worse, pleading. Use the *same command* each time you request a certain action (not "General, come" one time and "Come here, boy" the next). Keep things simple. Many trainers include the dog's name in all commands requiring motion (come or heel) but omit it from commands that require the dog to remain motionless (sit, stay, or down).

Immediately correct each improper response to a command with a verbal, "No!" Repeat the command, show the dog the proper response, and lavish with praise when successful. Try to keep your talking to a minimum. Use simple, clear commands and repeat them only when necessary. Your goal is to have the dog respond correctly in response to one command. If the dog needs constant prompting, it is not responding correctly and probably is confused about what you want it to do.

In training, slower is better. Each new lesson should build on the success of the previous lesson. Patience and consistency are the keys. Many repetitions will be needed before the dog truly understands how it is to respond to a given command. I believe that an act quickly learned is an act quickly forgotten, so progress to new exercises very slowly and check the dog often to be sure that it truly understands what it is to do.

Corrections are an important part of the learning process. The trainer must correct swiftly, fairly, and consistently. Patience is essential, as the correction should not be out of anger. In most instances, the dog is confused about what you want and is not misbehaving willfully. Shouting at or striking the dog only will make matters worse. This is a common mistake with rottweilers, as uninformed people feel a dog of this size needs extraordinary amounts of restraint and punishment. In reality, proper guidance and praise will encourage the dog to do well and make it more responsive to the will of the owner. Few rottweilers are bullied easily into submission by physical abuse. Such a dog never will be reliable, as it will be responding to commands simply to avoid more punishment.

Keep the lessons short and pleasant so that the dog will remain eager to learn. If you push the dog too hard, especially when things are going well, you run the risk of disinteresting it in the learning process. End each lesson with lots of praise and petting, and follow this with a pleasant activity, such as a walk or favorite game. This special attention lets the dog know you are pleased with its performance. With such positive reinforcement, the dog will learn to enjoy training rather than dread it.

Housebreaking

Housebreaking is probably the puppy's first real challenge. Therefore, owners must do their part in making housebreaking the puppy's first success. Remember: through success the dog learns confidence — both in itself and in you.

Housebreaking a rottweiler puppy can be accomplished quickly if the owner keeps close tabs on the puppy during the first few weeks in the home. The most important thing to know is *when* a puppy will need to eliminate: after eating, after waking, after strenuous play, the first thing in the morning, and the last thing at night. The puppy always should be taken to the elimination area at these times. Because a puppy has very limited capacity, it will need to go at other times as well, and it usually will give some physical clues that it needs to eliminate: it looks uneasy, sniffs the ground, and walks in circles, as if searching for something.

The elapsed time between a successful trip to the elimination site and "an accident" is short, so the owner must be alert. Quick housebreaking depends in large part on the attentiveness of the owner: monitoring and understanding a puppy's physical signs of impending elimination, getting it to the proper elimination area in time, and praising every success.

Housebreaking also is aided by the fact that dogs have an instinctual desire to keep their "den" area clean. This instinct already has been ingrained in the puppy by its mother. When a litter is young, the dam cleans up each puppy's eliminations by ingesting them. When the pups are no longer newborn, she no longer will tolerate their eliminating near the sleeping area. When the puppies soil the den, she corrects them and they soon learn to do it elsewhere. When a puppy is raised by its dam until weaned, it usually knows that some areas are acceptable for elimination and others are not. The new owner needs to build on this.

Until a puppy is at least four to six months of age, it has limited control and cannot "hold it" for long. "Accidents" are inevitable and the puppy should not be punished or hit. Above all, *never rub the puppy's nose in excrement.* Such acts will do nothing but confuse the dog and make matters worse. The owner should show displeasure by pointing at the spot and saying "No!" in a stern tone of voice. The owner must then give the puppy a clear indication of what *proper* procedure is by taking it to the elimination area and praising.

What do you do when you discover an "accident" has occurred while you were not with the dog? It is a common misconception to believe that a dog that skulks away from an owner who has discovered an unwanted deposit is feeling the pangs of a guilty conscience. In reality, the dog is exhibiting the typical signs of fear and confusion. It is running for cover, not feeling ashamed.

Dog trainers disagree on whether or not you can correct and discipline a dog for an act that you did not witness firsthand, but I believe that you can show a dog what displeases you if you make a "connection" in the dog's mind between the "evidence" and your surly reaction to it. Do not overreact when you find an unwanted deposit. You want to let the dog know you are displeased, but you need to show it exactly what you are displeased about. To make a connection in the dog's mind with your displeasure and the waste, bring the dog to the spot. Point at the excrement and have him look at it. Scold in a low, guttural tone. Immediately bring the dog to the proper elimination area. Praise the dog if it should go there. When you both return to the house, banish the dog to its sleeping quarters for a short "time out" and then clean up the mess. Case closed. By making the dog connect your displeasure directly with the excrement and the banishment, the dog has been shown that this act will not be tolerated — even when the owner is not present.

Thoroughly wash each "accident" site with a solution designed to specifically remove urine and excrement odors (available from veterinarians or at pet shops) or with a soapy solution containing a little vinegar. Do not use an ammonia-based cleaner, as this may reattract the dog to the spot rather than repel it.

Tips for Housebreaking Puppies

During waking hours a young puppy should be taken out almost hourly to be given a chance to eliminate. The more chances it is given, the more chances it has for success and praise — and nothing is more encouraging for your rottweiler than praising its good behavior. You will not have to keep this up throughout the dog's life, as the dog soon will get better control of its bodily functions, but paying a lot of attention to this task really is worth the effort. The number of required walks gradually will diminish to three a day when the dog reaches maturity. Don't rush the pace, however, because the pressured and punished puppy can wind up as a chronic soiler when mature.

Always accompany your puppy outside when it is time for elimination. You cannot just open the door, let the dog out, and expect it to eliminate. A puppy is distracted easily and most likely will spend its time outside playing. Later, it will relieve itself inside — much to the despair of the owner who "just took it out." During the training period the owner needs to instruct the puppy on where to go and, most of all, the owner must be present to lavish the puppy with praise when it succeeds.

Until the puppy is reliably housebroken its movements must be restricted. Instinctively a puppy does not want to soil its den, but it does not regard other places as highly. When not under direct supervision, the unhousebroken dog should be confined to either the sleeping area or the elimination area.

Select a small, uncarpeted, "puppy-proof" area for the sleeping area, and make sure that all escape routes are blocked off. A mesh baby gate will do well while the rottweiler is small, but it may not be high or sturdy enough when the dog has grown a bit. The elimination area should be outside, rather than a papered area in the house, if possible. Paper training is necessary only when an owner cannot be present in the home for long stretches of time during the training process. Crating is also a very effective method for housebreaking (see Crating Your Puppy, following).

Immediately bring the puppy to the elimination area whenever it shows signs of needing to go. Praise each success. When mistakes are made, show your displeasure so that the dog makes a connection with your mood and the "accident," and then immediately bring it to the correct spot.

By removing the puppy's water bowl at night and feeding only the prescribed amount of food (no snacks) on a regular schedule, the owner can help to regulate the dog's elimination needs. By controlling the puppy's intake, you can expect the bodily processes to be fairly regular as well, which will aid the owner in predicting when the dog will need to go.

Crating Your Puppy

Dog crates are effective training tools, and should not be regarded as cages or prisons. Dogs, as pack animals, instinctively will seek out the confinement and security of a den. When used properly, a crate becomes the dog's den, and most dogs regard it as a peaceful place to rest and relax. A dog almost always will sleep while in its crate. Most dogs adapt quickly to a crate and instinctively will try to keep this area clean by not eliminating in it. When paired with a regular schedule of walks and feedings, a crate greatly can aid the housebreaking task.

Crates come in a variety of sizes and material, so be sure to buy one that fits your needs. Most are made of either heavy-duty plastic or wire mesh and they can be purchased from pet shops and dog supply stores. The crate must be large enough for your rottweiler puppy to comfortably sit or lie down in, but not so large as to give the dog enough room to subdivide the space into a bed area and an elimination area. The bottom of the crate can be lined with a blanket for some additional comfort, or you can purchase a crate cushion from a supply house.

When devising a housebreaking program, put the puppy on a regular schedule. A growing puppy must be fed at least three times a day (at 7 A.M., noon, and 5 P.M., for example) and must be taken out frequently to be given a chance to eliminate. The crate can be used for brief periods between the walks, and as the dog matures the crating time can increase. A puppy has a very limited capacity to "hold it" and will be forced to relieve itself if confined for too long a time. This defeats the major benefit of a crate — to create an area for the dog in which it will not want to eliminate.

The owner must take the dog to its proper elimination area at regular intervals and enthusiastically praise the dog every time it relieves itself there. During the first few cratings the owner may want to remain in the same room with the puppy to help it feel at ease, but the owner should pay no attention to the puppy. If the puppy senses anxiety or guilt in its owner's behavior it may well act up to gain the owner's attention, or it may decide that the crate really is something to be afraid of because its owner obviously is upset by it.

During housebreaking start by crating the pup-

py for only 10 to 15 minutes at a time, gradually increasing the duration over the next few weeks. Physical needs vary from dog to dog, so the following schedule should be adapted as necessary to your particular rottweiler: during the day, puppies under 12 weeks of age may remain in the crate for up to one hour; puppies 12 to 16 weeks of age may be crated for up to two hours; older puppies may stay a maximum of three to four hours; all ages can be crated overnight.

The location of the crate is important. Place it out of the direct line of household traffic, but not somewhere that will make the dog feel isolated. You can give the dog an unbreakable nylon bone to help relieve any boredom, but don't give it small chews toys, which can be torn easily into chunks by an excited rottweiler and then choked on. Bowls of food or water do not belong in the crate during the housebreaking process.

Once the dog is fully housebroken, many owners feel that the crate no longer is needed. However, many dogs appreciate having such a den and will continue to return to their open crate for naps.

Paper Training

Although it is most efficient to forgo the use of papers and teach the dog to go directly on the outside, paper training is an effective method for those who cannot be with the puppy for long stretches of time during the day. Because most rottweilers will not gain enough bladder control to last through the day until approximately six to twelve months of age, papers probably will be required during this time unless access to the outdoors is provided. Outdoor training still should be encouraged, and working owners should walk the dog just prior to leaving each morning and as soon as they arrive home. A brief walk at midday, if possible, would be helpful.

An unhousebroken puppy always should be confined whenever it cannot be supervised direct-

Training Your Rottweiler

ly. Provide it with only enough space to have three separate areas: an elimination area, a feeding area, and a crate or sleeping area. If given too much room, it will not feel compelled to use your selected elimination spot. Cover the elimination area with several layers of newspapers, making sure they do not extend into the other two areas.

Whenever you think the dog needs to eliminate, and every time the dog seems agitated, place it on the papers. Stay with the puppy and encourage it with "Do your business, General" or any similar phrase that does not include the terms *come, sit,* or *down*, which will be used later as basic obedience commands. Praise the dog enthusiastically whenever it uses the papers. It should learn quickly that this spot is acceptable for elimination—and that you are pleased when it goes there.

To help reattract the dog to the elimination site, place a small piece of previously soiled paper on each new stack of newspapers whenever you change them.

Paper trained rottweilers will adapt to using the outside when they are mature enough to wait for access and when they are shown that they are supposed to use a new elimination spot. Shrink the size of the newspaper pile until it is small and then remove it entirely. You can help the transition by placing a small soiled patch of papers outside a few times to familiarize the dog with the new elimination spot.

Cleaning Up Waste

Quite frankly, dogs do not give a second thought to their wastes, once deposited. Therefore, the clean up task is the owner's responsibility. In many cities, owners who do not clean up after their pets can be fined from $25 to $500. Cleaning up dog waste not only rids the streets and public areas of repugnant and potentially harmful materials, but also proves that dog owners have good manners.

"Pooper-scoopers" designed for picking up

waste can be purchased from pet stores, or the task can be accomplished easily—and sanitarily—using just a plastic bag: Invert the bag so that it covers your hand, pick up the waste using the bag as a shield for your fingers, cup your hand, and invert the bag once more. The waste is now inside the bag, which can be placed in the nearest suitable container.

The Collar and Lead

You can familiarize a puppy with the feel of a collar on its neck by having it wear a lightweight collar, but no collar really is necessary until the dog is ready to begin formal obedience training. At that time your rottweiler will need a training or "choke" collar, which consists of metal links with a ring on each end. Due to this breed's strong, muscular neck, you may need a double strand choke or a training collar designed especially for the large breeds. This will depend on the dog's responses to the corrections.

The training or "choke" collar must be placed on the dog so that the chain connecting to the free ring passes over the dog's head.

A choke collar should be worn only during teaching sessions. It allows you to apply as much pressure as necessary to evoke the correct response or action by the dog. When pulled upward the collar momentarily will tighten around the dog's neck. Once the pressure is released, the collar immediately will loosen. The dog quickly will learn that an upward tug indicates displeasure and that a correction is needed. The choke collar is a teaching aid and it never should be used to inflict pain.

A choke collar should be the correct size for your dog—not one it will grow into. A correctly fitting collar measures approximately 2 inches (5.1 cm) more than the diameter of the dog's head. Because a choke collar is designed to provide quick, snap-tight corrections, it is pointless to buy oversized collars because they will not close quickly and can, in fact, be dangerous if allowed to hang loose.

To form the collar, slip the chain through one of the rings. The lead will attach to the free ring. The side of the chain connecting to the free ring must be placed *over* the top of the neck, not under. In this position the collar will release instantly whenever the upward pressure is released.

If you want your dog to wear identification, select a lightweight collar to which you can attach a small metal medallion listing the dog and owner's names, address, phone number, and any health problems the dog may have. Such name tags soon may become obsolete, however, as a new "high tech" identification system has been invented in which a tiny microchip containing information on the dog and its medical history is injected just under the skin at the base of the dog's neck. A hand-held scanner held over the chip will pick up the microchip's information, which then can be decoded by a computer at the central registry that records the specific information on the dog. Humane society shelters and veterinarians are being given free scanners in the hopes that more lost animals each year can be identified accurately and returned to their owners. The injec-

tion procedure is painless for the animal and the chip is embedded permanently. The procedure costs approximately $40, and there is a nominal annual renewal fee to keep the dog in the national registry.

Training leads are made of either nylon, woven cloth, or leather and come in various lengths and widths. Most trainers suggest a sturdy 6-foot (1.8 m) lead, 1/2 to 1 inch (1.3–2.5 cm) in width, although a 3-foot (.9 m) lead sometimes is used when more control is necessary and a longer line will be needed for teaching recalls.

Never allow the dog to chew the lead. Correct with a firm "No!" and give the lead a light upward tug to remove it from the dog's mouth. Many puppies are taken aback by the feel of this new weight around their neck, so you may want to let the puppy drag the lead behind it for a while. Remain close by to make sure the puppy does not get tangled and hurt, however.

If your rottweiler seems comfortable with the lead, pick it up but apply no direct pressure on the dog's collar. Follow the puppy wherever it goes for a few minutes, and then let the pup know it is time to reverse the pattern. Introduce the feel of a light upward tug whenever the puppy pulls on the lead. The puppy may be stunned by this intrusion, or even annoyed. Verbally reassure it in a calm, natural tone of voice that there is nothing to be afraid of (but do not pet it), and continue to apply the pressure whenever the puppy wanders out of your control area. The puppy should learn quickly that its actions are indeed under restraint and that the tugs require a corrective action.

The Basic Obedience Commands

With a breed as powerful as the rottweiler, the owner has a responsibility to his family, his dog, and the community at large to fully train and supervise the dog. This is not limited to the first few weeks in the home, either, but rather is a responsibility the owner must take on for as long as the dog is a member of the family. From the earliest days in the home, the owner must establish control over the animal by monitoring its actions and correcting all misdeeds in a manner that makes it clear to the dog what is not acceptable and what is the correct course of action. The rottweiler is not the right breed for the timid, uninterested, or absent owner.

Rottweilers have a tendency to be stubborn about obedience training, but they can be capable learners if the owner knows how to get the dog's attention and interest. Formal obedience training from a trainer experienced with this breed is recommended for all but seasoned owners. The trainer should be effective, but he or she does not need to be overly rough with the dog. Some of the most influential trainers base their methods on positive experiences for the dog, not on harsh disciplinary techniques. Inexperienced trainers often punish a rottweiler's mistakes too severely, basing their treatment on the dog's size, strength, and reputation. A good handler can control and train his or her dog through verbal reprimands, physical corrections, and effective instruction, but this takes experience with the breed.

The owner of a rottweiler cannot consider his or her dog as trained until it will obey every command instantly, given only one command. This cannot be a hit-or-miss situation, where the dog obeys *most* of the time. The dog must be reliable *every time* it is called on to obey your command. Accept no less, as a rottweiler will try to get away with a less-than-perfect performance once you begin to permit it.

Every rottweiler must learn at least five basic commands: "sit," "stay," "heel," "come," and "down." I consider these the necessary manners a dog must have if it is to live well among humans. The following descriptions of the basic obedience exercises will aid in your instruction. They serve only as outlines, as there are as many methods used in practice as there are trainers. Because every dog responds differently, your task is to find the method that works best for you and your particular dog.

To enhance the dog's concentration, begin by practicing only indoors in a quiet area free from distractions. The dog should be on lead for all the basic exercises.

Sit

The formal "sit" calls for the dog to sit at your left side, with its shoulders square to your knee. Position the dog at your left side, and hold the bulk of the lead in your right hand. Keep the lead taut and apply some upward pressure to help keep the dog's head up. If your dog is responsive to your motions, you can lead it into the sit by raising your left hand over its head and moving your hand back toward its rear as you command "Sit." If the dog follows your motion, it naturally will fall back into a sit. More often you will have to help it. Place your left hand on the dog's rear as you command it to "Sit" and press firmly down until it is in the sitting position. When the dog moves out of

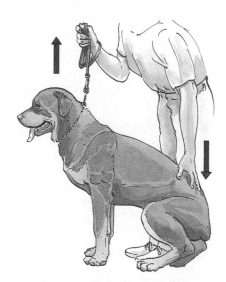

When teaching the "sit," apply upward pressure from the lead in your right hand as you press downward on the dog's rear with your left hand.

position, use your left hand to straighten it; your right hand continues to supply the moderate upward pressure from the lead.

Praise the dog highly and give it a few pats when it is positioned properly. It is important to praise the dog when it *reaches* the sit position, not when it gets up because it must learn to associate your praise with the sitting action. Release with "Good boy!" and/or an upward sweep of your left hand (the sweep is used in later, more advanced exercises).

During the first few lessons keep the sits quite short. In this way the dog has little chance to fall out of the proper position or lie down. Gradually increase the time the dog is to sit, and whenever the dog moves out of position correct with "No!" and a light jerk from the lead, then immediately put it back in place.

Rottweilers take quickly to this command, and you should not need to press on the rear long before the sitting action becomes habitual in response to the command. Once your dog is performing the "sit" reliably, you can move on to the "stay" and "heel" commands, which build on this.

Stay

It is foolish to rush ahead and begin work on the "stay" if the dog is not performing the "sit" reliably. In all training, slower is better.

Begin training the stay by placing the dog in a sit, keeping some upward pressure on its neck from the lead in your right hand. As you command "Stay!" simultaneously take one step away from the dog, using your right leg (which is the farthest from the dog) to step off. Bring the palm of your left hand down toward the dog's face, stopping just short of its muzzle, in time with the command and the step. Retain eye contact, if possible (but many rottweilers feel threatened by constant eye contact, so do not insist on a stare-down between you and the dog). As soon as you anticipate movement by the dog, repeat the command while maintaining the signal.

The "stay" is taught with the dog in the sit position. As you command "Stay!" extend your palm toward the dog's face and move away a short distance.

Your rottweiler undoubtedly will try to move toward you once it sees you move away, or it will try to lie down. When the dog breaks the stay, return it immediately to the sit and repeat the whole procedure. Ten seconds is enough time for the first stay attempts, so release the dog quickly and praise.

The stay involves a lot of self-restraint on the dog's part, so be patient and do not expect immediate results. Correct each infraction and try again, but do not bore the dog with endless repetitions. The stay should not be practiced continuously. Spring it on the dog every now and then, and praise each little success lavishly.

Top: The rottweiler is a well-rounded breed that excels at ▶ retrieving games. Bottom left: The retrieve complete, the rottweiler relaxes in the sun. Bottom right: Whenever your dog finishes swimming, make sure it is dry down through the dense coat to the skin to prevent a sudden chill.

As the dog shows signs of understanding the stay command, slowly extend the length of the stay and the distance you move away from the dog. Once the dog thoroughly understands the command, it will be able to stay in the sit position for several minutes at a time.

Heel

I view the "heel" as an absolute necessity, as it makes walking with your dog an enjoyable pursuit rather than a painful or exasperating experience. Heeling is simply a controlled walk, and every rottweiler should be required to perform it. An untrained rottweiler often will surge ahead on the lead, pulling the owner along for a ride. Alternatively, it may lag behind or veer off to the sides whenever it finds an interesting scent to follow. Such bad habits cannot be tolerated and must be stopped while the dog is young.

The first few minutes outside should be allotted for elimination and investigation. Once the dog loses that initial thrill to be outside, you are ready to set off.

Your rottweiler should always walk on your left side, its chest preferably in line with your knee. Hold the lead in your right hand and use your left to supply corrective jerks when needed. Begin with the dog in a sit. Step off with your *left* foot, commanding "General, Heel!" as you move forward. If the dog does not follow you instinctively, give the leash a tug to start it forward. Remove the pressure from the lead whenever the dog responds and remains in proper position.

Walk at a pace that is comfortable *for you* and jerk the lead only if the dog strays from position.

Make your snaps quick and firm and repeat "Heel!" with each correction. Praise the dog as soon as it responds, using a pleasant tone and "Good dog!" Repeat the praise every now and then as you are moving if the dog remains in position, but don't overdo it as this can interfere with the dog's concentration and confuse it about what you are praising.

If you aspire to any obedience competition, the dog will be required to sit at your side whenever you stop. Many owners do not require this of their dogs, but I feel it is a good action to ingrain because it always keeps the dog in close proximity and tight control. In the beginning you will need to issue the sit command whenever you stop, but as the dog becomes adept at the procedure the sit will become automatic and no verbal command should be needed.

Learning to heel takes time, and you can count on your rottweiler to lose interest frequently at

You must teach your rottweiler to heel when walking. The objective is a well-behaved dog that does not lunge forward and pull you along.

◀ This dog exhibits the fearless expression and attentive gaze that is legendary for the rottweiler.

remaining at your side. Every time the dog breaks from position, stop and place it in a sit. You should not have to endure continually snapping the dog back into position. By placing the dog in a sit you allow it to succeed at a task it already knows, and therefore it can be praised. Without this break, there can be a lot of leash corrections and not much praise administered. Resorting to the sit will help the heeling practice continue rather than break down into confusion on the dog's part and anger on the trainer's. Once the dog successfully has completed the sit, step off again with "General, Heel!" and repeat the procedure.

Whenever the dog strays significantly from the proper position, you must break this pattern by stopping for the sit. If not, you will be applying continuous pressure from the lead on the dog's neck. In this way the choke will become meaningless and frustrating to the dog, and possibly physically damaging. The choke is to be used sparingly to regain the dog's attention and bring about a correction in the form of a sharp, upward tug. It is to be used only when needed and should be released immediately. Rottweilers are extremely muscular around the neck and oftentimes are impervious to the snap of the standard choke chain. If this is the case with your dog, you should consult a professional trainer for guidance on selecting a more effective training collar that is appropriate for the breed.

The initial heeling lessons should last only 10 to 15 minutes. When the dog becomes more adept and no longer needs the frequent corrective sits, you can lengthen the heeling lessons as energy and interest permit. Once the dog becomes accomplished at heeling, your time together during walks will be infinitely more pleasurable. You must also take care to instruct and proof the dog on how to react to other people and animals that it may encounter during these walks.

Come

Once it has adapted to the sound of its name, a puppy will almost always happily come when called in anticipation of something pleasant. As the dog matures, it encounters a few unpleasant experiences and its responses sometimes become more reluctant (I call this the "What's in it for me?" syndrome). The "come" teaches a dog to control its urges and obey its master's call regardless of the circumstances, without hesitation.

Rottweilers instinctively will respond to the sound of their master's voice and seek it out, and this is a valuable tool when training for the come. Begin the training period with some pleasant play. The dog should be roaming on a long lead or rope (20 feet [6.1 m] or more works best) in the practice yard, with the trainer holding the lead but maintaining only minimal tension. Once the dog is relaxed and preoccupied, command "General, Come!" and lightly snap the lead to start the dog moving toward you. Praise when the dog *begins* to move. Have the dog come directly to you and place it in a sit.

It is the owner's responsibility to teach the dog how to walk peaceably on the leash—regardless of the distractions.

If the dog does not respond to the tug, give the lead a snap and repeat "General, Come!" Should the dog stubbornly resist, repeat the command once more and calmly reel the dog in by slowly retracting the cord. Once it reaches your side, place it in a sit.

Release the dog with "Good dog!" and let it roam once more. Practice the come intermittently, enforcing the command with a sharp tug on the lead whenever the dog fails to move immediately toward you. Test the dog on the come no more than once or twice each training session, but do not hesitate to use the come at various times throughout the day when you *really want* the dog to return to your side. Do not use the command if you are not in a position to enforce it, however. The main points to remember are that you must praise the dog highly when it comes when called and that you must *never* allow the dog to ignore the command.

The owner must use this command responsibly. *Never command the dog to come to you and then punish it when it arrives.* When you see your dog doing something wrong, *go to it* and administer the correction. Should you command the dog to come and then punish it when it arrives, you almost certainly will ruin your chances of having a dog that will return to you instantly when called.

Down

The "down" is a very useful, sometimes life-saving command. Do not attempt to teach your rottweiler the down until it is reliably performing the "sit" and the "stay."

Begin by placing the dog in a sit, with you kneeling by its side. As you command the dog to "Down," grab its front legs near the body, gently lift them from the floor, and lower the dog to the floor. Once down, command the dog to "Down, stay!" (Remove the "stay" part of the command as soon as the dog begins to understand the concept.) A very responsive dog can be enticed to drop its front down through just hand motions beginning under the dog's chin and arching down to the floor and out in front of the paws. It is useful to incorporate a down motion with your hand at the time of the command, especially if you intend on continuing into obedience competition.

Praise with "Good dog" once it reaches and remains in the prone position. Rest your left hand on the dog's back to deter it from rising, should it appear ready to pop back up. Release the dog after a few seconds by motioning upward with your hand and gently tugging the lead. The dog should then return to the sit position.

The downward movement is the concept that the dog needs to learn and this must clearly be differentiated from the stay. Do not make your dog remain in the down position too long at first, and be sure the dog remains lying on all fours. The dog is to be alert in this position, not sprawled over the floor.

Practice the down several times each day. As the downward drop becomes more familiar, try issuing the command and just slapping the floor with the palm of your hand to get the dog moving down. If you still encounter a reluctant response, try placing the lead under your left foot, keeping it rather taut, and as you command "Down!" add a slight pressure on the dog's shoulders to get it moving down.

Once the down becomes a natural movement for the dog, teach it to lie down on the lead from various positions (such as in front of you or from a distance). When working indoors, practice the down off the leash. Never accept a sloppy performance once the lead is removed, however. Oftentimes, the dog may not feel compelled to obey once it realizes that the lead is no longer attached. Such behavior is, of course, unacceptable.

Down-Stay

One of the most effective methods of controlling your rottweiler in various situations is through use of the "down-stay," an exercise combining two of the commands discussed above. With practice your dog will remain in a down-stay for 30 minutes or more, enabling the master to remove the dog from those activities it is not invited to participate in or to keep it from getting underfoot without having to lock it up. The down-stay teaches the dog self-discipline, and enforces the trainer's position as leader.

Select a spot that is out of the way, yet not secluded, and tell the dog to "Down, stay." The owner should remain nearby to monitor the dog, but should not pay too much attention to the dog during the process. Begin with stays of a few minutes and gradually increase the time, but vary the length of the stays so that the dog cannot anticipate when the exercise will be finished.

During the initial attempts your rottweiler undoubtedly will try to break the stay. As soon as it *begins* to move, tell the dog "No, Stay!" and replace it. End the down-stay with an "Okay" and an upward sweep of the hand, and lots of praise. This exercise requires a lot of self-control on the dog's part, and does not come easily to a rottweiler, but through practice and praise it can be mastered. Its usefulness cannot be overstated.

It is perfectly acceptable to let the dog sleep during the down-stay as long as it remains where it was placed when it awakens. You need to formally complete the exercise, however, to be sure it has an impact, so wake the dog by tapping your foot near its head or gently slapping the floor in front of its head when it is time to release the dog.

Training Problems

The rottweiler was developed for its working ability and has been shown over many generations to be an exceptional companion and mighty guardian. This heritage underscores the trainability of these dogs, but these images must be balanced by the fact that this is also a very assertive breed with a noted stubborn streak.

Rottweilers are at their best when given proper instruction and guidance, as they want to please and work with their owner, but each dog and owner is an individual with strengths and weaknesses. There are as many training methods as there are people teaching dogs, and some methods work better than others. Some dogs learn more quickly than others. Some trainers are more persuasive than others.

Various problems can arise during training that interfere with the learning process. Your dog may not be able to adapt to the training method you have selected. Finding the solution to a training problem generally is a matter of trial and error and, most of all, patience and perseverance. With a breed as assertive as the rottweiler there is often a need to call upon the expertise of a trained professional.

When you encounter a training problem, step back a bit and evaluate your teaching technique. Are your commands clear, concise, and consis-

A dog the size of a rottweiler should *never* be allowed to jump up on visitors. To discourage this habit, raise your knee the instant the dog starts to jump. Catch it midchest as you correct with a firm "No!"

tent? Are you rushing the dog rather than giving it ample time to learn? Do you speak in a firm, authoritative tone, or do you shout, scold, or whine? Do you praise the dog with every success?

By observing the dog's behavior and body language during training you may get some clues as to the cause of the problems.

Is the dog easily distracted? You may need to train in a more secluded training site and see if its concentration improves. Alternatively, the dog may be too young to begin training.

Are the training problems a new occurrence or constant? A sudden disinterest in training or confusion in a male can be caused by a local bitch in heat. A temporary learning plateau commonly occurs for both dogs and bitches during the fifth or sixth week of training that makes it appear as if the dog has forgotten all it has learned. This odd phenomenon generally passes in a week or so.

Is the dog ill? A dog that is reluctant to move freely or jump may be showing the early signs of hip dysplasia. A dog in pain also may reflect this in excessive aggressiveness. If the dog shows any

of these tendencies have it examined thoroughly by a veterinarian.

Control is a must when dealing with a rottweiler. If you feel things are not progressing well, it is best to consult a professional trainer who is experienced with this breed. Oftentimes an expert quickly can detect an underlying problem and propose corrective measures. Many times a new approach or technique that the dog will understand or like better will correct the problem. Sometimes the owner needs instruction in how to keep the dog's interest or discipline the dog effectively.

Training setbacks are inevitable and must be countered with patience. The owner of a rottweiler can expect a certain amount of feistiness on the part of the dog, for it is in its nature. A danger arises if the owner counters each problem with anger and hostile treatment, as this can have a detrimental effect on the future training of the dog. On the other hand, if the owner despairs and gives in to the will of the dog there is the added danger that it will end up uncontrollable and aggressive. Should things deteriorate, *seek help from a professional*. It is money well spent.

Breeding Quality Rottweilers

Typically, when a breed skyrockets in popularity — and demand quickly outpaces supply — there is an inevitable breakdown in the quality of the puppies being produced, as unskilled breeders try their hand at "cashing in" on the boom. Luckily, this has not affected the rottweiler breed on a large scale. Due to the work of careful breeders, the incidence of hip dysplasia (a predominantly genetic disease) has in fact declined in rottweilers in recent years. It is my fervent hope that this trend is not reversed by too many random breedings.

With a powerful breed such as this, it is vital that all rottweiler puppies be produced from parents with stable temperaments and sound conformation. Breed integrity will be maintained only if matings are carefully planned events, using quality animals.

A skilled breeder does more than just produce puppies; he or she is dedicated to producing puppies that are of equal — and hopefully *better* — conformation quality than the parents. A breeder works hard to select the best possible breeding partners in the hopes of producing the best possible offspring. The American Rottweiler Club, the national breed club, publishes the "A.R.C. Statement of Principles and Practices," which includes 11 guidelines for breeders. Highlights include:

• Breed only AKC registered dogs and bitches which are . . . OFA-certified. . . . All dogs should be tattooed . . . before having hips x-rayed.

• Offer as stud, with a contract, only mature (two years of age or older) healthy dogs with normal hips, free of communicable diseases. . . .

• Breed only bitches two years of age or older with normal hips, in good health, free of communicable diseases. . . .

• Sell only to responsible persons and refuse to knowingly deal with unethical breeders, pet shops, wholesalers, catalog houses or their commercial sources. . . .

The sections that follow outline some requirements for formulating a sound breeding program. If you are interested in breeding your rottweiler, you should read one of the in-depth manuals on dog breeding available in libraries, bookstores, or pet supply shops. The added details in these manuals will help with the many day-to-day aspects of breeding. Raising quality puppies is a full-time job, with long hours of work and a considerable investment of money. It is not a "get rich quick" activity, as many people believe.

Selecting a Sire and Dam

A breeder's most important decision is which sire and dam to use. Each potential sire and dam should be evaluated in terms of their strengths and faults, as compared to the breed standard. The more a breeder knows about the dogs in the previous generations of these dogs the better; a dog's outward appearance is the result of the set of genes it received from its parents.

The selection is complicated further by the fact that a dog's outward appearance is no guarantee of its ability to pass on its traits to its offspring. Every dog may have hidden traits that are not expressed physically, but that can be passed on. The trick is to select quality dogs with a pedigree containing quality genes that have been passed through the generations. Experienced breeders can determine this by reviewing pedigrees for traits that have been expressed consistently in succeeding litters of puppies.

Novice breeders mistakenly assume that breeding a conformation champion to another champion will produce a litter of future champions. This may or may not work. Although the sire and dam each may be of superior conformation, each may carry genes for traits that do not complement their partner's. The resulting puppies are often of lesser conformation quality than the parents.

The brood bitch forms the basis of a breeding kennel. It usually is very difficult to buy a top-quality bitch puppy from an established breeder, who naturally will be reluctant to part with a promising female puppy. Many novice breeders therefore begin with a quality-producing *adult*

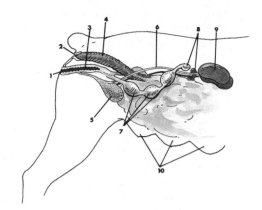

The reproductive organs of the rottweiler female:
1. vulva
2. anus
3. vagina
4. rectum
5. bladder
6. ureter
7. developing embryo
8. ovaries
9. kidneys
10. mammary glands

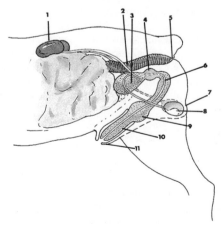

The reproductive organs of the rottweiler male:
1. kidneys
2. rectum
3. bladder
4. prostate
5. anus
6. urethra
7. scrotum
8. testes
9. bulb
10. penis
11. sheath

bitch from an established kennel. This eliminates the uncertainty of breeding a maiden bitch, but proven producers usually are quite expensive (if you can even find a breeder that will part with one).

When selecting a stud, the emphasis is on finding a dog that will enhance and complement the specific qualities of the bitch. An experienced stud that already has produced quality offspring is, of course, preferable. A good rottweiler stud should be the correct size, balanced, and a good mover, and have a good coat and pigmentation, sound temperament, and proper bite. He should be as free of obvious faults as possible, and his weakest points should be in areas where your bitch is strong.

You will need to review the pedigrees of all dogs being considered for a mating to see if the two dogs share any common ancestors. If a pedigree was not supplied when you purchased your dog, ask the breeder to reconstruct this information, as it is very useful in determining from which type of breeding system your dog stems.

Beginners should seek the advice of an experienced breeder whenever possible. He or she will be better able to evaluate the faults and strengths of the potential sire and dam, and later the quality of a litter.

Breeding Systems

There are three basic types of selective breeding systems: *linebreeding, inbreeding,* and *outcrossing.*

Linebreeding

Linebreeding is the practice of mating dogs that stem from the same family lines but that are removed from each other by at least one generation (for example, dam to grandsire, cousin to cousin, sire to granddam). Linebreeding enables a breeder to "fix" correct type by strengthening desirable traits that already are present in a line.

Linebreeding also limits the flow of undesirable genes into the breeding stock, as dogs exhibiting undesirable traits are eliminated from the breeding plans.

Inbreeding

Inbreeding is the practice of mating closely related dogs, such as sister to brother, daughter to sire, or dam to son. Because no new genes are introduced by unrelated partners, such a mating intensifies the genes already present in the bloodline.

When used by knowledgeable breeders, this system can quickly fix type and bring uniformity to desired traits in a line. However, it also can enhance any faults in the line. Faults that had been unexpressed as recessive traits are more likely to be expressed in inbred animals due to the limited number of possible gene combinations. These faults ultimately can be eliminated, however, as those animals exhibiting or carrying the trait would be removed from the breeding program.

Inbreeding can be an effective method when used sparingly by knowledgeable, experienced breeders. It is used rarely in successive matings and usually is combined with linebreeding techniques.

Outcrossing

Outcrossing is the practice of mating dogs that do not share common ancestors in the first five generations. An outcross is used to eliminate faults by pairing dogs that hopefully will complement each other's faults. Each is selected because it has shown itself able to pass on the quality traits the partner lacks.

Outcrossing is not random selection. For example, a stud from a line known for good fronts would be chosen for a bitch from a line possessing good proportion and size but weak fronts. Hopefully the resulting offspring would retain her good points and acquire his good fronts. Outcrossing adds new genes to the bloodline, rather than intensifying ones that are present already.

Outcrossing typically is used when linebreeding fails to correct a particular fault. The breeder then selects a line that is thought to be complementary to compensate.

The random selection of dogs of the same breed technically is outcrossing, but for the purposes of this discussion that type of indiscriminate mating would not be considered a true breeding system. Unstructured outcrossing is the usual pattern for "backyard breedings," which usually do little except produce puppies of lesser quality than the proceeding generation. These matings must be frowned upon if the genetic quality of the rottweiler breeding stock is to be maintained.

Preparing for Breeding

Rottweilers are slow to mature, so it is recommended that a bitch or dog be at least two years old before being used in a breeding program. The partners in a mating must both be in good physical condition. The bitch should be examined by her veterinarian approximately 30 days before her heat cycle or "season" is expected. At that time he or she can evaluate the bitch's health and determine if any inoculations or controls for internal or external parasites are needed. Both dogs also should be tested for canine brucellosis, a highly infectious disease that results in fertility problems.

Mating

The beginning of the bitch's heat cycle is marked by a noticeable swelling of the vulva, which becomes hard to the touch. A watery discharge that may later become tinged with blood soon follows. The bitch will be ready for mating on approximately the tenth day after the onset of the cycle. In the early days of the cycle, she is attractive to males but will not allow coitus. Ovulation generally occurs around the ninth day into the cycle, after which time she is fertile.

Mating often involves dogs from different kennels. The female usually is brought to the dog for most stud services, as females generally adapt quickly to a new environment and are not as easily unnerved by strange surroundings as males.

Two or more handlers should be present during the mating to assist the animals and keep things calm. The bitch often is muzzled to prevent a sudden snap at the stud or handler. The stud mounts the female from the rear, his front legs resting around her middle. Once penetration and ejaculation have occurred, a section of the stud's penis will swell and the two dogs will be "tied" together for a period of up to 30 minutes. The handlers should supervise the dogs until the tie is broken naturally. Any attempt to force a break of the tie can have serious consequences for both the stud and bitch. To ensure a successful fertilization, the bitch generally is bred again two days later.

Pregnancy

Gestation in dogs generally is 63 days, although the puppies often arrive a few days earlier. There is little physical evidence of pregnancy during the first few weeks, although the dam may have a better-than-average appetite during this time. An experienced breeder or veterinarian can feel the puppies at approximately four weeks after mating, but an owner never should try to feel for puppies during this time, as this can cause serious damage to both dam and puppies. The dam's abdomen should begin to show signs of pregnancy after five weeks.

The dam must be fed a high-quality diet throughout the pregnancy. Supplementation rarely is needed in the first five weeks, but she will require additional calories (primarily in the form of protein) during the last weeks. She should be fed smaller, more frequent meals as the pregnancy progresses (three or four a day) to alleviate the discomfort of a large meal.

The dam should be encouraged to carry on with her normal daily routine and to exercise

throughout the pregnancy, as she will need strength and good muscle tone for an easy delivery. Do not allow any vigorous exercise or pulling during the last two weeks, and discourage her from climbing stairs.

The dam should be introduced to her whelping box in advance of her delivery date. Be sure she has time to investigate and become comfortable with it before delivery, or she may choose her own spot to have the puppies. The whelping box must be placed in a warm, dry, draft-free location that is not a high-traffic area.

An appropriate box can be purchased from pet stores and supply outlets or constructed at home. It must be large enough for her to deliver the litter in and to raise the puppies for several weeks. She should be able to lie on her side and stretch out, but the box should not be so large as to allow the puppies to crawl too far away from the warmth of the mother. The sides of the box must be low enough to allow the dam to easily come and go, yet high enough to keep the puppies confined while small. To prevent the dam from inadvertently crushing a newborn against the side it is advisable to place a "guard rail" several inches in width on the sides of the box. The bottom of the whelping box should be lined with layers of newspaper, which can be removed easily when soiled.

Delivery

Approximately 24 hours before delivery the dam will become restless and her temperature will drop to around 99°F (37.2°C). She will slow down her activities and seek out her "nest" when labor pains begin and delivery nears. She may become agitated and will begin to pant heavily. She may vomit. A novice bitch will be very anxious at this point, so praise her constantly. It is important that you remain calm, as she can sense apprehension and may become panicked if she senses your fear. Notify your veterinarian that whelping time is near, so that he or she will be ready if an emer-

Breeding Quality Rottweilers

gency should arise. Inexperienced breeders should also ask a more knowledgeable breeder to assist in the delivery. If you do not have an experienced breeder to assist, get a thorough briefing from your veterinarian on the entire delivery process prior to whelping time.

Needed supplies include washcloths, a heating pad, blunt-tipped scissors, waxed dental floss (for tying the cord), a scale, paper towels, a wastebasket, and a lined box or bed to place newborns in while others are being born. All supplies should be purchased well in advance of the delivery date and placed in the whelping area.

The first puppy generally takes the longest amount of time to arrive. It will be encased in a membrane sac, which must be removed if the newborn is to begin breathing on its own. Should the bitch fail to tear the sac open and cut the umbilical cord, be prepared to perform this task for her. An afterbirth normally should be expelled within several minutes of each birth. Do not be alarmed or surprised if the bitch eats an afterbirth, as this is quite normal and will not harm her. You must make sure that all afterbirths have been expelled. If any appear to be retained, contact your veterinarian.

A typical rottweiler litter will contain from six to eight puppies, but larger litters are not uncommon. Allow the dam to lick and suckle each newborn, but remove the already born when the delivery of the next puppy begins. During this time gently wipe the newborn clean, weigh it, and place it temporarily in a heated holding box until all deliveries are over. Record the facts of each delivery (time of delivery, sex, weight, any physical abnormalities), and, if necessary, mark the puppies with various ribbons or dots of nail polish to tell them apart.

A rottweiler brood bitch will have a gentle touch with her puppies. She will have a tolerance for onlookers, but she may become annoyed if constantly interrupted by new faces or loud noises. Give the new mother a lot of praise and offer her a warm drink of broth once the final pup-

py has been expelled. A first-time mother should be monitored closely over the next few days to be sure she shows a healthy interest in her litter. If she should become disinterested, agitated, or aggressive with the puppies, seek immediate veterinary assistance for her and guidance on how to care for the puppies yourself.

Caring for Newborn Puppies

The dam will care constantly for her new litter over the next four weeks, but she will leave the whelping box during this time for exercise and meals, and to occasionally clear her head! The puppies will receive enough antibodies from the dam's colostrum (the first milk) to protect them for the next six to ten weeks from most of the common contagious diseases. They then will require their first battery of shots to continue the protection.

For the first few weeks of life the whelping box must be kept in a warm spot (approximately 85° to 95°F (29.4°–35°C)). Puppies are not physically able to keep themselves warm when very young, so their body temperature rises and falls in accordance with that of the immediate surroundings. Most breeders are unable to adjust the entire holding area to this elevated temperature, so they opt to keep the room at from 70° to 75°F (21.2°–23.9°C) and add additional heat (in the form of covered water bottles, heating pads, or infrared bulb lamps) to the whelping box. With this method you must monitor the box constantly, as the puppies easily can become overheated and possibly burned. They will be much better able to regulate their heat at about five to six weeks of age.

The dam will attend to all the basic needs of the puppies while quite young, and you should not try to dissuade her. Aside from feeding them, she will also stimulate them to urinate and defecate and then clean up by ingesting their wastes. This will not last forever, however, and she will begin basic manner training of her litter when they begin

Breeding Quality Rottweilers

A well-constructed whelping box has ample (but not excessive) room for the dam and her litter, and it is easily cleaned.

nosing about and trying to tumble out of the box.

The owner's main job during the first few days is to attend to the *dam's* needs, and to keep the whelping box clean. On each visit to the whelping area check to see that all puppies are accounted for, nursing well, and that none have strayed from the warmth of the mother. Each newborn should be picked up and checked regularly for overall health and its weight gain should be recorded daily. If any puppy does not thrive by the third day, consult your veterinarian.

Rottweiler puppies often are voracious nursers, kneading with their paws against their dam's teats. By two to three weeks of age their nails can be rather sharp, and they may scratch — and annoy — the dam. If this is the case, the owner should trim the puppies' nails carefully with baby scissors.

The owner should shower the rottweiler puppies with love — not overdoing it, of course — in the first two weeks. Newborns can be stroked gently, caressed, and softly spoken to from birth to begin the human-dog bonding process. The puppies' eyes will begin to open at 10 to 14 days, but it will take another week or so before they can focus properly. The puppies begin to hear at

around 12 to 17 days, and soft music and human cooing and stroking is good stimulation for them.

At approximately three weeks of age the puppies can get their first dose of "solid food." At first, add just a small bit of gruel to some formula — and get the cameras ready for some priceless shots of when the puppies dip their heads into their bowls for the first time. This weaning process begins the puppy's transition to adulthood, and rottweiler puppies should get lots of attention at this time.

By frequently handling each puppy and talking softly to it, the owner helps socialize the dog on how to react toward humans. A daily brushing with a soft brush also will help accustom the puppy to this process, and that will make it more willing to be touched throughout its life.

Rottweiler puppies seem to have abundant amounts of energy, but they tire easily. The early visits with the puppies should be short and sweet, being sure that the dogs do not get overexcited. The puppies should be allowed this time with dam and littermates, as they will learn some valuable lessons on life.

Weaning is the first step toward adulthood — often a very messy step!

Useful Literature and Addresses

Rottweiler Breed Clubs

American Rottweiler Club
General Information
  Doris Baldwin
  P.O. Box 23741
  Pleasant Hill, California 94523

Judge's Education
  Jan Marshall
  College Hill
  Woodstock, Vermont 05091

Rottweiler Club of Canada
  Rural Route 2
  Cochrane
  Alberta TOL OWO
  Canada

Schutzhund Clubs

North American Working Dog Association
  1677 N. Alisar Avenue
  Monterey Park, California 91754

United Schutzhund Clubs of America
  3704 Lemay Ferry Road
  St. Louis, Missouri 63125

International Kennel Clubs

American Kennel Club (AKC)
  51 Madison Avenue
  New York, New York 10038

United Kennel Club
  100 East Kilgore Road
  Kalamazoo, Michigan 49001-5598

Canadian Kennel Club
  2150 Bloor St. West
  Toronto, Ontario M6S 4VT
  Canada

The Kennel Club
  1-4 Clargis Street Picadilly
  London W7Y 8AB
  England

Australian National Kennel Council
  Royal Show Grounds
  Ascot Vale
  Victoria
  Australia

Irish Kennel Club
  41 Harcourt Street
  Dublin 2
  Ireland

New Zealand Kennel Club
  P.O. Box 523
  Wellington, 1
  New Zealand

Organizations

American Boarding Kennel Association
  4575 Galley Road
  Suite 400A
  Colorado Springs, Colorado 80915

American Society for the Prevention of Cruelty to
  Animals (ASPCA)
  441 East 92nd Street
  New York, New York 10028

American Veterinary Medical Association
  930 North Meacham Road
  Schaumburg, Illinois 60173

Canine Eye Registration Foundation
  South Campus Court, Building C
  Purdue University
  West Lafayette, Indiana 47907

The Delta Society
  P.O. Box 1080
  Renton, Washington 98057

Humane Society of the United States
  2100 L Street, N.W.
  Washington, DC 20037

Orthopedic Foundation for Animals (OFA)
  2300 Nifong Boulevard
  Columbia, Missouri 65201

Useful Literature and Addresses

The Seeing Eye
  P.O. Box 375
  Morristown, New Jersey 07963

Therapy Dogs International
  P.O. Box 2796
  Cheyenne, Wyoming 82003

Books

In addition to the most recent edition of the official publication of the AKC, *The Complete Dog Book,* published by Howell Book House, Inc. in New York, there are:

Alderton, David. *The Dog Care Manual*. Barron's Educational Series, Hauppauge, New York, 1986.

Baer, Ted. *Communicating with Your Dog*. Barron's Educational Series, Hauppauge, New York, 1989.

Frye, Fredric. *First Aid for Your Dog*. Barron's Educational Series, Hauppauge, New York, 1987.

Klever, Ulrich. *The Complete Book of Dog Care*. Barron's Educational Series, Hauppauge, New York, 1989.

Lorenz, Konrad Z. *Man Meets Dog*. Penguin Books, London and New York, 1967.

Smythe, Reginald H. *The Mind of the Dog*. Thomas, Bannerstone House, London, Great Britain, 1961.

Ullmann, Hans-J. *The New Dog Handbook*. Barron's Educational Series, Hauppauge, New York, 1985.

Index

Aggressive behavior, 5
Air travel, 20–21
"Alpha" figure, 54
American Boarding Kennel Association (ABKA), 22
American Kennel Club (AKC), 5, 6, 7, 44
Anal glands, 40
Anatomy, 50
Appearance, 6

Bathing, 29
Behavior patterns, 47
Boarding, 21–22
Body language, 47–48
Bonding, 75
Bones, 25, 26
Breed club, 7, 76
Breed standard, 50–53
Breeding, 5, 8, 13, 70–75
  systems, 71–72

Canine socialization period, 12
Car, riding in the, 19–20
Cats, 17
Chewing, 26
Children, rottweilers and, 6, 17
Coat, 29, 52–53
Collars, 59–60
Come, 66–67
Commands, 55
  basic, 60–68
  verbal, 6
Communication, 47–48
Conformation competition, 5, 8, 49
Constipation, 39–40
Corrections, 6, 55
Crates, 20, 57, 58

Dam, 11, 12, 14, 54, 72
  selecting, 70–71
Delivery, 73–74
Diarrhea, 39
Doghouses, 19
Dog walkers, 18
Down, 67
Down-stay, 67–69

Ears, 37
Elderly, rottweilers and the, 6
Elimination area, 57
Emergency care, 41–45

Evolution of dogs, 44
Exercise, 7, 18–19, 49
Eyes, 31–32

Facial expression, 47
Fear biters, 48
Feeding process, 25–26
Feet, 33
Fences, 7, 19
Fighting, 17
Fleas, 36
Food, 23–26
  canned, 24
  dry, 23
  semimoist, 24

Gestation, 73
Grooming tools, 29–30

Health care, 31–43
Health examination, 31
Heel, 65–66
Hip dysplasia, 40–41
History, 44
Homes, 7
Hound glove, 29
Housebreaking, 23, 56–59
Human socialization period, 12

Identification, 60
Inbreeding, 72
Injuries, 41–42
Internal organs, 38

Kennels, 6, 11, 19
Kindergarten Puppy Training (KPT), 18

Leashes, 60
Lice, 60
Life span, 6, 14
Linebreeding, 71–72
Littermates, 12
Litters:
  neighborhood, 8
  size, 74

Madden, John, 5
Males, 7
Mating, 72–73
Maturity, 8, 49
Medication, giving, 34–35

Motion sickness, 20
Muzzle, emergency, 41

Nails, trimming, 30

Obedience competition, 5, 49
Obedience training, 6, 54–55, 68–69
Odors, removing, 57
Omen, The, 5
Outbreeding, 72
Outcrossing, 72
Ovulation, 72
Owners, 6–7

Parasites, 35–38
Paper training, 58–59
Pedigrees, 71
Perceptions of rottweilers, 5
Personality, 5, 6, 49
Pet-quality, 8, 13
Pet stores, 8
Pets in the home, 17
Poisonings, 42
Praise, 55
Pregnancy, 73
Price, 8
Pulse, taking the, 34
Puppies, 7
  age to purchase, 8, 12
  early lessons, 54–55
  evaluating, 11
  feeding, 16, 25
  first day in home, 14–15
  first night, 16
  housebreaking, 57–59
  introducing, 16–17
  lifting, 15
  newborns, 74–75
  selecting, 11
  supplies for, 14
Puppy socialization classes, 18
Purchase agreement, 8, 12–13
Purchasing a rottweiler, 6–11
Purebred Dogs: American Kennel Gazette, 7

Registration papers, 8, 13
Registration statistics, 5, 44
Reproductive organs, 71

Schutzhund, 5, 49

Index

Seasons, 7
Selecting a rottweiler, 7, 13
Sex, 7
Shedding, 29
Show quality, 8, 11, 13
Sire, 11, 70–71
Size, 6, 50, 51
Sit, 61–62
Skeleton, 52
Sleeping box, 14, 16
Socialization, 18
Spaying, 7
Standard, breed, 51–53
Stay, 62–65
Stinging insects, 38
Stud dogs, selecting, 70–71
Supplements, 24–25

Supplies, basic, 14

Tapeworms, 36
Tattoos, 22
Teething, 26
Temperature, taking the, 34
Territoriality, 6
Therapy work, 5, 49–50
Ticks, 37
Tooth care, 32–33, 43
Tracking, 5, 49
Trainers, professional, 5, 48, 61
Training, 48, 54–69
  housebreaking, 56–59
  problems, 68–69
  and puppies, 54–55
  rules for the trainer, 54–56

Traveling, 19–21
  by car, 19–20
  by plane, 20–21

Vaccinations, 35
Veterinarians, 5
Vomiting, 39

Weaning, 75
Weight, 6, 50
Weight-pulling competition, 49
Whelping, 73–74
  supplies, 74
Whelping box, 73, 75
Who should own a rottweiler, 6
Worms, 36